Third and Long

Men's playbook for solving marital/relationship problems and building a winning team

ADVICE FROM A GUY WHO LEARNED THE HARD WAY

By Steve Campbell

www.thirdandlong.ca

1663 LIBERTY DRIVE, SUITE 200
BLOOMINGTON, INDIANA 47403
(800) 839-8640
WWW.AUTHORHOUSE.COM

© 2005 Steve Campbell. All Rights Reserved.

No part of this book may be reproduced, stored in a retrieval system, or transmitted by any means without the written permission of the author.

First published by AuthorHouse 12/21/04

ISBN: 1-4208-1810-4 (sc)

Printed in the United States of America
Bloomington, Indiana

This book is printed on acid-free paper.

DISCLAIMER
This book was written to inform, educate and expand the awareness of its readers. No one involved in the writing or publishing of this book is a physician, mental health professional, or accredited marriage and relationship counselor, although members of these professions have been consulted on many aspects of the material. Neither Steve Campbell nor the publisher nor any of their associates shall be liable or responsible to any person or entity for any loss, damage, injury or ailment caused, or alleged to be caused, directly or indirectly, by the information or lack of information contained in this book.

CONTENTS

Acknowledgments .... **iii**

Personal Note from the Author .... **iv**

Chapter 1: Introduction and Overview
Time for men to stop faking relationships 1

Chapter 2: Relationships
It's a whole new ballgame 5

Chapter 3: Assessing the Players
You 15

Chapter 4: Assessing the Players
Your partner 25

Chapter 5: Assessing the Team
You as a couple 37

Chapter 6: It's Third and Long
Time to get serious 59

Chapter 7: Where Do We Go from Here?
Start with the fundamentals 61

(continued)

Chapter 8: Your Relationship Playbook

More tips and techniques 81
- A. THE BIG STUFF 84
- B. DAY-TO-DAY PLAYS 93
- C. GIFTING/ROMANCE 99
- D. THE PHYSICAL SIDE 108
- E. COMMUNICATING 114
- F. CAUTIONARY TIPS 121

Chapter 9: Your Game Plan

Building Your Unique Playbook 129

Chapter 10: It's Game Time

There is no "I" in team 133

Closing Comments 135

Appendix: Recommended Reading 136

About the Author 138

Notes 139

ACKNOWLEDGMENTS

It's been said that most non-fiction books are written by authors standing on the shoulders of those who have gone before them, and this book is no exception. *Third and Long* relies heavily on the many academic researchers and bestselling relationship authors who have uncovered and publicized important findings in relationships and marriages over the past few decades. I express gratitude to these many professionals for their outstanding work.

I also wish to thank the friends and relationship experts who took the time to review the manuscript and offer thoughtful comments and suggestions. In particular, relationship counsellor Jim Skinner provided guidance and mentorship during many stages of the book. Most importantly, my ex-wife Jane Keyes provided invaluable editing and typesetting assistance that helped this book achieve its final shape; I can truly say this book would not be in its present form without her help.

However, while I thank all these people for their assistance and support, responsibility for this book's final contents and opinions rests solely with the author.

Steve Campbell

PERSONAL NOTE FROM THE AUTHOR

It could happen to any man.

This book has its roots as both a confession and as a warning. Looking back, the mistakes I made in my marriage seem to be from somebody else's life. Was that really me? Yes, I have to admit it was, and as it turned out I graduated with honors from the School of Hard Knocks.

Sadly, I'm not alone. Writing this book has helped me to understand where I went wrong and how to change for the better — and most importantly to move on with my life. Now I try to embrace the upside of what happened — i.e., the learning/personal growth opportunity — yet it still bothers me when I see other guys making the same dumb-ass mistakes I made. That has been my biggest motivation in writing this book.

What started out as an account of my mistakes (and more than a few of them are listed in this book) has developed into a tool that I hope will help other guys save their marriages — or just have a much better relationship than they have now. Reliving what happened to me will have been well worth it if it can help others be more successful.

The relationship know-how men need

It's time for men to get better at relationships. This is a "how-to" playbook that provides the know-how you need to excel in your personal relationships — without having to resort to reading book after book. It's designed to help you begin understanding right away what makes your woman tick and identify in specific ways what she wants. And, more importantly, it addresses how you can keep her content and invested in the relationship so that you can have your cake and eat it too — in a relationship that's far more enjoyable than what you have now.

Relationship = Team

Underlying the strategies presented here is the analogy that a relationship is much like a sports team, in which all players work together to win. For many men relationships are difficult to understand, but mention the words "team" and "teamwork" and they instantly gain a sense of what needs to be done. Hence the main theme of this book: just as winning in sports requires hard work, building a winning relationship team demands a substantial commitment of time and effort. And, as in sports, success is achievable — if you work smarter, not always harder.

Yet the football analogy has its limits. The old-school Vince Lombardi paternalistic coach-as-dictator approach is out, even in today's hard-driving NFL. Players today would never stand for what one former Packer said about Lombardi's coaching style: "He treats us all like dogs." Similarly, the top-down hierarchy in marriage is over. Yelling and barking no longer works. Equality is the new standard in relationships.

In making use of the sports analogy, it might be useful to think of marriage as an offensive line, where the linemen work together to build a great unit. In sports it's often the working together toward a goal — win, lose or tie — that's the most fun. It can be the same in marriage.

Unlike sports, this is a win–win situation

For some guys it may appear that improving relationship skills is a win–lose scenario — meaning that when you focus on building relationship skills your maleness is downgraded: you are emasculated. In fact, the opposite is true. Adding these skills into your repertoire builds on your existing strengths and enables you to become a stronger person and a better man, because you can now relate more effectively to women — and, come to think of it, even to children and co-workers. It's absolutely a win–win situation.

More to the point, there's a good chance that, rather than diminish you as a man, these expanded skills will give you more time to be just that. How so? First, your efforts in the relationship will become much more focused, and thus much more effective and productive. You may get higher-quality results this way because your efforts will have a greater positive impact on your partner. Second, she could become so happy with you that she may reward your efforts by pushing you out the door to go enjoy yourself, her resentment having ebbed away.

Thus, developing better relationship skills could actually give you more time to do "guy" things (like hunting, fishing and playing sports). Of course, there is also the possibility that you end up enjoying the relationship so much that you decide to spend even less time with the guys. Whatever the outcome, you won't be complaining if the result is increased happiness in your relationship and your life.

Guys, it's not our fault

This is not about finding fault. It's about getting better at something — which we all should have done long ago. After all, it's not as if guys sit around all the time discussing their relationships in great detail as, apparently, a lot of women do. And our dads didn't sit around with their friends and sons and talk about their marriages either. This book is a tool designed to help you get up to speed quickly on relationships and go deeper than many guys ever do.

Note to women

In general men are not socialized to do the right thing in relationships. To overcome this "disability" for a greater good (i.e., to love you the way you deserve to be loved), they need to "fake it 'til they make it." That is, to choose to do things that don't come naturally so that, over time, these behaviors will become reflexive, even pleasurable. Through this process, many men will come to truly know themselves and their own capabilities. In the beginning, however, this is best done by practising or acting out the role they eventually hope to make a "natural" part of their romantic playbook.

For you, the key message to be taken from this book is that, if your man only knew how important many of these behaviors were to the future of your relationship, he might choose to get as passionate about them as he is about football — if only because your contentment is central to him and the future he has in mind. This book highlights the need for men to develop foresight, to learn to pay attention to tiny signals, and to stop believing that "good enough" is good enough. Most importantly, it provides him with a selection of easy-to-implement skills that he can put into action immediately.

I believe that most men, given the knowledge of how important the relationship is to you, will want to surface their attitudes (understand how they really feel about you and the changes they need to enact) and adjust their behaviors (alter how these attitudes are exhibited in everyday life) because they truly love you. And, if they decide to rise to this challenge, the chances are excellent for improving the connection and happiness in your relationship.

This book also explains in simple terms to men the risks they face in the relationship game if they don't take on this challenge. After reading this book, they can't say they weren't warned or didn't know what to do.

Who should read this book:
Sons, nephews, brothers, husbands and boyfriends

All men have "coachable" moments in their lives: times when they're especially ready for new ideas on how to live better and excel in their relationships. Some of these coachable moments include when a young man has his first serious girlfriend, when he gets married, when he becomes a father, and at any point in a man's life when he senses there might be more to an experience than he's achieving. This last opportunity can occur at any age; the first three are very specific instances. The information in this book can help in all these situations.

As we continue to witness the breakdown of marriages of five, ten, twenty and thirty years' duration, who cannot help but wonder: am I next?

While it's important to reinvigorate existing marriages, consider this book a how-to guide for your sons, nephews and male friends on building a winning relationship right from the start.

Good versus bad manipulation

One final word about manipulation. There are two kinds of manipulation in this world. The good kind leads to open and rewarding relationships, the other to deceit and one-sided relationships destined to fail. This book shows men how to manipulate their relationship skills and techniques and marriage with the intention of helping them achieve a greater good in our society: the emergence of stronger, more loving equal relationships. Equality leads to intimacy. Intimacy leads to justice, which leads to greater happiness — the winning ingredient for success in the relationship game. (What a concept — if only such information had been available to me!)

It's game time, so let's get started.

Steve Campbell
Vancouver, B.C.

CHAPTER I

Introduction and Overview

Time for men to stop faking relationships

———————————— ✳ ✳ ✳ ————————————

Women fake orgasms and men fake relationships.

This candid comment from actress Sharon Stone is a sad but all too true commentary on the state of many marriages and relationships. However, the reality today is that fewer and fewer women are willing to grin and bear the fake relationships and orgasms their mothers accepted. Men must become better at the game of love, fast.

Often the biggest disaster in life for a man — far worse than losing his job — is losing the woman he really cares about due to his own negligence or ignorance. Yet, every day, every week, every month and every year, it happens to smart, reasonable guys. The shock of your wife or girlfriend suddenly up and leaving hurts like a punch to the stomach. I can vouch for this.

Many men are unprepared for relationship breakdown

The steam of a number of seemingly unrelated events gathers and there is an unexpected explosion. Hindsight helps many men to see the signals they didn't catch at the time.

So your relationship seems a bit off, or your wife appears distant. There's something wrong but you can't get a handle on what it is. Some of the greatest failures in history have occurred in cases where the information on an approaching catastrophe was there (Pearl Harbor and 9/11), but wasn't interpreted properly or in time to prevent disaster. It's the same with relationships. The signs are often obvious — if you're looking for the clues and taking the time to assemble the pieces of the puzzle.

Don't think it can happen to your marriage? Comedian Joan Rivers said it best: "Half of all marriages end in divorce — and then there are the *really* unhappy ones." There are approximately one million divorces each year in the United States and Canada. Assuming it takes five to ten years for a marriage to gradually break down, there could be up to ten million marriages on the road to separation and divorce right now. Add in those many millions of relationships with a thread of unhappiness running through them and the odds are pretty good — especially if you're reading this book — that your marriage may be a candidate for breakdown. Is yours currently in the "just okay" category? Or is it much worse than that?

Analyzing a woman's game plan

The good news is that relationship breakdown doesn't have to happen. Women are as easy — and complex — to read as the baseball box scores in the papers. This sounds paradoxical, but consider: for the uninitiated, that box score is indecipherable. For those in the know, however, it requires little or no concentrated effort to understand. Women can't help but communicate how they are feeling and what they want (sometimes in more detail than perhaps you'd like). You just have to be tuned in to their signals.

Ironically, many women spend their lives trying to camouflage these signals to make them less obvious. That's why other women can understand what a woman's plans are, while a man may not. They speak The Language. And so can you, but only if you pay careful attention.

It is no wonder, then, that it's women who are most tuned in to relationships and buy related books. In fact, most are aimed at females because they are the ones who will seek help proactively in order to protect, repair or enhance their key relationships — with their spouse, their kids, their friends — while men tend to be reactive and not think about their relationships until presented with a serious problem.

Hence, when things go sour, men are often on the receiving end of the "surprise." In fact, more than 60 per cent of all divorces are initiated by women, while under one-third are led by men. These are staggering statistics. And aiming all these books at women is highly ironic, as it skirts the number-one problem in relationships: the emerging need for *men* to develop advanced understanding, insight, awareness and skills.

> Men aren't entirely responsible for relationship troubles

This book is titled "Third and Long" because a majority of men don't react to a problem until it has reached a crisis point. The good news is that, as in football, third and long is just a mini-crisis within the overall big game. There's still time to change tactics and end up with victory. What's interesting in the marriage game is that many men don't realize how close at hand defeat may be: simply because they're legally wed or living common law for years, they assume their partner is content and will honor her lifetime contract. Unfortunately, it turns out that contracts, like promises, are sometimes broken.

Obviously, men aren't entirely responsible for relationship troubles: it takes two people to make togetherness work. Yet it's reasonably clear that most men are deficient in some or many relationship skills. And, with rare exceptions, they can't put the responsibility for relationship breakdown on their spouse until they have mastered these skills. At that point and only then can men begin examining women's role. Until then, men need to focus on catching up — or risk losing out in the relationship game.

The reason for this new state of affairs is that women of all ages in modern society are now in a stronger position to ask for what they want: better, more intimate relationships. They are demanding more from men and moving on if men can't or won't make the effort. Unlike previous generations, many women are now unwilling to settle. Men who want their relationships to continue must address this "relationship gap" — end of story. They need to become considerably more relationship-savvy, and there's no time to waste. Read on for some targeted tips that can be implemented right away.

CHAPTER 2

Relationships

It's a whole new ballgame

--- ✳ ✳ ✳ ---

Bride, *n*. A woman with a fine prospect of happiness behind her.
— Ambrose Bierce, *The Devil's Dictionary*, 1911

The good old days — the way the game used to be played
The good old days were never really as good as they sound today. (Just imagine what sex was probably like back then and you'll get the idea.) Still, there's no question men used to have it pretty good in their affiliations with women. Here's a snapshot of the way things were for generations of marriages, until it all started to crumble around the last generation.

In the good old days — let's call them the "John Wayne Era" — the man was the provider and protector. In football terms, he was the all-powerful coach or quarterback. Like the characters John Wayne portrayed, he was typically strong, silent, and the keeper of his wife, children and property. He was in charge and his wife supported him. Of course, she used female persuasion and "nudges" on him from time to time to get the family's need met, but for all intents and purposes the man was the head of the household: dominance unchallenged.

The wife's singular role was to take care of the home while her husband brought home the bacon. She took charge of the kids and the running of the house, and made sure his drink and slippers were ready when he came home after a long day at the office or factory.

In sex, the most important thing was making sure he was satisfied. For many men, this was the extent of their expertise about sex. And wives were onside with this arrangement; they too believed their needs were secondary. Besides, the topic of sex and women's sexual response was taboo. The pill was not yet available and women were often relieved just to have sidestepped spinsterhood. Boy, have times changed.

In the John Wayne Era, children were expected to be seen and not heard. Dads didn't talk much to their kids and, when they did, they often didn't have much to say.

Sound familiar?

Since Dad was supreme in the household and no challenge was permitted, kids mostly just tried to keep out of his way. He didn't really get involved in teaching his sons how to be men or showing his daughters what to expect from a decent man.

Dad also didn't talk much to Mom, except to clarify his needs and concerns. Her requirements for support and communication were not considered important, except perhaps in times of emergency. Looking back, Dad was really just a family figurehead, a cigar store Indian looking good in front of the store but not truly involved. And while the character stereotype John Wayne represented won some battles in the movies, overall he doesn't sound like a very fun guy to hang around with — for his wife, his children or his friends.

Women in the John Wayne Era had very few options. Essentially, they were dominated by their husbands and had little say over their own lives. It was not a time when women fulfilled their dreams.

Although these stereotypes are being exaggerated to illustrate the point, believe it or not that was generally the way of marriage back in the "good old days." Just ask your mom or aunts who are in their sixties and seventies now; your dad and uncles, on the other hand, might respond to such queries with a self-interested "no comment." If you were to observe closely, you might discover that this state of affairs still exists for many of those couples wed in earlier decades and entrenched in these stereotyped roles.

> The days in which the man ruled the roost are over

What's truly amazing, however, is that many younger men still hope that parts of this myth can be their relationship reality today. Sorry, boys, the game has changed. The days in which the man ruled the roost are over.

Women have changed forever
Women hope men will change after marriage but they don't; men hope women won't change but they do.
— Bettina Arndt

It's all happened so fast over the last few decades that many men don't truly understand how much women have changed. The good old days are gone and they aren't coming back. It's a whole new ballgame. Today, men must grow and change in marriage or suffer the consequences.

For instance, these days most women can provide for themselves, and some bring home more money than their husbands. A wife is just as likely to work outside the home, while increasing numbers of husbands are adopting the responsibilities of childcare and home administration.

Women have also broadened their horizons. Your wife, for instance, may dress up a lot for work. She may even get hit on at the office. Her tastes and interests have expanded. She no longer cares which dish soap cuts the grease best or makes her fingernails shine — in fact, she expects her husband to be washing a significant share of those dirty dishes.

> Today's woman is demanding more than her mother received

She has her own tastes in music and movies, enjoys fashion, and loves to get together with her friends. Today's woman has seen the world, and once you've been to Paris or New York it's hard to be truly happy cleaning behind the refrigerator.

In sex she expects quality attention. The '60s revolution and the introduction of the pill make her satisfaction in the bedroom as important as her man's. Her husband is no longer her whole world. She's in charge of her own destiny; to put it succinctly, she now has options.

Given those options, doing his laundry, ironing his clothes and cooking his dinners day after day are not exactly stimulating alternatives. Cooking can be drudgery or a labor of love at best for many women, especially with an audience composed of thankless children and a husband who might not even seem to notice the effort. Maybe she'd rather order in, leaving more time to fulfill her own hopes and dreams.

TV has further broadened her exposure to the outside world. She's no longer isolated in the home, waiting for her husband — her world — to come home and give her life a purpose. (There is some debate about whether this was ever the case but — what the heck — I'm presenting the male viewpoint here.) At any rate, she and her friends know exactly what's happening, and increasingly they're choosing to make it happen. Today's woman is demanding more than her mother received.

You could call this "women's liberation," but it's not about bra-burning, it's about women realizing they have power in their lives and marriages and that their fundamental need for vital, quality relationships is legitimate. There's no coming back from this kind of liberation, because you can't take back reality. They want the best and they're going to get it.

In defense of men, progress has been made since the 1950s. There is definitely more equality in relationships today — or, perhaps more accurately, less inequality. Women's needs in sex are more front and center. She has her "girls' nights out" and he might be into cooking a bit and cleaning up the house occasionally.

What men don't seem to get, however, is that this emerging equality is just the tip of the iceberg. (You might be surprised to know that many women find it highly comical — and sometimes infuriating — that we men expect praise for these "favors" we do for our wives!)

Many women outgrow John Wayne

Another point to remember today is that many young women may lack confidence in taking on the world. One result of this is that they may actually embrace the John Wayne relationship model (the man as protector and provider) in their younger years while they figure out how the world works and their place in it. However, once they've gained confidence and experience (typically by their late 20s and into their 30s), the John Wayne model quickly becomes too restrictive. They've outgrown the stereotype and as a result the bargain they struck — inequality or subservience for safety and financial support — isn't looking so good anymore.

This is where men's frustration often arises. What happened, some ask, to the days when she was happy to have me take care of her? Remember when being a wife and mother was all she wanted out of life? Who changed the rules without any notice?!

In a nutshell, she did. And, even more surprisingly, she's making no apologies for it. By invoking the universal female right to change her mind at any time, essentially she's offering you a choice: grow and change with her or else risk losing her. Guys, the bottom line here is that if she begins to reject the old provider/protector model, you have to adapt to this new reality if you want to keep her.

Today, from the woman's point of view, her rights now include a relationship that contains passion, communication, attraction, humor, caring, spontaneity and excitement — things that may not be abundant currently. Not getting them can lead to her expressing general or specific feelings of dissatisfaction. Or worse.

Now this can be extremely perplexing to men, because according to the John Wayne model many were brought up with — and to which she initially agreed — she has everything she needs. Plus, maybe he's also bringing home lots of money to keep her in a good lifestyle. So why are the waters suddenly getting choppy? Men might ask the question, "What is the problem with women?"

The problem today is not women

Frankly, it's not. It's men's relationship skills and experiences in society: they simply have not kept pace with the rapid emergence of women's needs for deeper relationships — ergo, a new and serious relationship gap. There's no shame in it, though. It's all come on so fast in the last decade or two that men just need to do some catching up. Sadly, this lack of skills means, for many men, that their relationships begin eroding the moment they move in with a woman, simply because they don't know how to build and maintain the bond in a way that ensures the woman will stay attracted and passionately involved for many years. Again, if this is the case, don't feel alone: an informal survey of your male friends will probably reassure you that you're in substantial company.

Part of the problem is that men implemented their dad's simplistic John Wayne Era marriage at a time when that marriage model barely worked with their mother's generation, never mind for younger women with

> The upside is that individual men can solve their personal relationship problems right now with a well-organized game plan and a little bit of teamwork

higher expectations. Or, men take the examples they see in old movies and add them into their marriage mix. To worsen matters, once the novelty of being married wears off many men try to resume the lifestyle they had before they tied the knot, leaving women to assume a role much like that of their mothers. No wonder women are rejecting this setup.

Overcoming these entrenched relationship traditions is a lasting societal issue that may take a couple of generations or more to resolve completely. The upside is that individual men can solve their personal relationship problems right now with a well-organized game plan and a little bit of teamwork.

Most relationship counselors agree that men are going to have to start pulling their share of the load, because the current reality is that if women had to choose between having a high-quality, fun relationship or a big house with two cars in the driveway, most would choose the relationship. And that's a scary thought for any man who senses that something may not be right in his relationship. Could this be you?

For individual men, the personal problem of how to do the right things in a relationship — although at first seeming incredibly complex, perhaps even mystifying — is not insurmountable. It ranges in complexity somewhere between throwing a baseball (easy) and mastering an effective golf swing (hard). Viewing it from a sports perspective may help.

There's an old saying: "Taken by the yard, life can be hard. But taken by the inch, life can be a cinch." As in sports, by breaking the problem down into reasonable, easy-to-implement components, men can analyze and tackle individual skills and tips and become a master at each level before moving on to the next. Just as they learned how to shoot a puck or nail a three-pointer, men can learn the fundamental and advanced skills needed to build an incredibly successful marital team. That's good news given that today's woman is moving forward rapidly — if necessary without her man.

Time to develop relationship skills

Men only evolve with a gun at their head.
— Screenwriter Paul Rudnick, *The Stepford Wives*

The new relationship reality is pretty clear: it's third and long and, as screenwriter Paul Rudnick notes, the gun is at men's heads. As much as many guys wish they could go back to the John Wayne Era (in which they headlined the show), it's time to give up on that fantasy. Men must get more skilled at relationships if those relationships are to continue and thrive. It's only recently that women have begun relating to men on a more equal footing economically and socially. Now men have to decide to move level with women on the emotional front.

What is your level of "want to" in the relationship

For a man, part of improving his relationship skills includes learning how to understand and analyze himself, his wife and their relationship team. This will help him decide how he really feels and what he wants (or doesn't want). Once that awareness is achieved he can implement many strategies aimed at conveying to his wife how much he loves her. But first he must determine his level of "want to."

There likely is little doubt you love her — that's why you're reading this book. You just need to get better at letting her know and making her feel loved. Sounds easy, doesn't it? Just buy flowers once in a while and you're homefree. Wrong. The process requires much more involvement than that. This is the central lesson I learned the hard way, and the one I most hope to pass on to other guys. The huge upside is that you've probably been underachieving so much that the improvements you do make will leave her feeling you're her personal Brad Pitt, Mel Gibson, Robert Redford or — what the heck, pick your generation — Cary Grant. So, rest assured, there's plenty of payback for the work you're about to put in.

First let's take a look at where you, your wife and your relationship are at right now.

CHAPTER 3

Assessing the Players

You

--- ✻ ✻ ✻ ---

Before you make a move you must assess the situation. In sports the coaches figure out an opponent's strengths, weaknesses and tendencies. They view film. They study previous games. They analyze the performance of the other team. As former Arkansas basketball coach Nolan Richardson said in his five Ps of sports: "Preparation prevents piss-poor performance."

Similarly, rebuilding your marriage involves preparation: scouting, to determine where you, your partner and your relationship are at. Once you figure that out you can make decisions and begin to detail a game plan for how to proceed.

One of the most important decisions for you in this section is to decide how much you want to rejuvenate your involvement in the relationship. Knowing what you really want and communicating it can be a hugely attractive feature to your partner. Here's a question to guide your thinking: how far am I willing to go to make this relationship successful?

What exactly is it you want?

You need to get a handle on this. Figuring yourself out is the foundation for making good decisions about how to improve your relationship with your wife or girlfriend. Should you stay and fight for it, or cut your losses and move on? How do you really feel?

More to the point: who are you and what do you really want? Do you truly want to be with her? Look deep in your heart. Clearly, there are troubles, or you wouldn't be reading a relationship book.

Do those troubles exist because there are things about her that bother you? Do they annoy you a lot? These may be little things, but there may also be bigger issues. Or are *you* the problem? While the little things won't kill a marriage, added together they can sink it. The big things taken individually can do that all by themselves.

You know what the biggies are: lack of communication, disrespect, different interest levels in sex, opposing attitudes about money or socializing, different beliefs about child-rearing. The smaller but still serious irritations for her might revolve around your playing/watching sports and drinking (enjoyable guy things, without question), or your wanting to spend more time with your buddies rather than painting the living room, playing with the kids, or taking a walk down the beach with her. Maybe from your viewpoint she's demanding and a perfectionist; perhaps she's untidy, forgetful or conceited.

Know what you really, really want

First and most important, you must decide what you truly want. Is this woman really for you? Last time I checked they weren't handing out more years of your life. Do yourself a favor and get the most out of it. Be honest with yourself. The tips in this book for enhancing your relationship are irrelevant if she's not for you and you just wish she'd get out of your life. Let's face it, some guys — hell, many guys — are just treading water, happy to have someone to cook and wash clothes for them and keep the kids out of the way while the game's on.

Well, to repeat, the days of the little woman washing your dirty shorts until you're sleeping on the wrong side of the grass are close to ending. More likely, you'll be cleaning your own shorts by the time that's even close to happening. As I've said before, women now have options and they're willing to exercise them. If you use this book just to fool her, you might get a couple of more years out of your relationship — but she'll punt you eventually.

> At issue is whether you are being authentic

So, back to you. Do you want to stay with this woman for another ten years, if not your lifetime? If so, you need to really understand what that will take.

Are you being authentic?

First you need to be honest about it, first and foremost to yourself. Women have superb B.S. detectors, and they'll eventually find you out if you're lying. (And lying isn't the way to go anyway. Lies are too difficult to remember, plus they set you up for living a dishonorable life. Worse, eventually they come back to sack you.) So if you're not interested in this relationship, you're better off admitting it sooner rather than later. This is a tough but important thought to ponder.

At issue is whether you are being authentic. If you're not being real in the relationship, she'll spot it from a mile away. What do I mean? The test of authenticity is this: can you be yourself when you're with her? Do you like who you are? Do you look forward to being with her? Or, instead, do you find yourself trying to pretend you're someone else in order to fit in with your partner? Do you feel manipulated or manipulative? The answers to these questions will help you make decisions later.

EXERCISE
Getting to know yourself
Before we move on, find out how well you know yourself by answering some targeted questions. These are the kind marriage counselors often ask. Try to be completely honest.
- Do you feel as if you are just "playing" the husband role?
- How comfortable do you feel on a day-to-day basis?
- Do you have any close friends with whom you have shared negative feelings about your relationship?
- How well do you get along with your parents and siblings? What are their opinions about your relationship?
- What are the three things you like most about your wife?
- Do you believe you got married for the right reasons?
- It's been said there are four rings in marriage: the engagement ring, the marriage ring, the nose ring and the suffering. Are you in the last, terminal stage of marriage? Is there any hope for the two of you?
- Honestly, now, answering just to yourself, do you really like your wife as somebody actually to spend a lifetime with? Or is it a chore? Perhaps it feels more like a life sentence than a life? Is it even worth the bother?

If you think it's a chore, well here's another revelation: you're probably as much or more of a bother for her. In fact, she is likely well ahead of you on the road to detachment and separation. What she doesn't know (unless you have already been brutally honest with her) is whether you don't like her *for certain*. If she did know that, well, pass the butter, because you'd be toast.

The fact is that you may not be suited to your wife. So, rather than go through the exercise of trying to make your marriage work, maybe you're better off cutting yourself from the team. Realizing this can be sad, but also liberating.

Someone once said, "The only thing I regret about all the mistakes I made in my life is not having made them sooner." What does this mean to you? When you fast-forward to the end of your life can you foresee feeling this way? If so, then the sooner you admit you have made a mistake in choosing your current partner, the sooner you'll be able to meet someone you can really connect with — take a moment or two to imagine how good that would be — and allow your wife to find somebody who can truly fulfill her needs.

Think for a minute about the aunts and uncles we all have (maybe even your parents) who stayed in their marriages "for the kids" or because they were afraid to leave. What kind of a life have they led, wasting decades with someone they didn't love, or worse, could barely tolerate. This sets an extremely bad example for children.

One way to look at your marriage troubles is that separating, although painful, can be the road to a better life. The more quickly you can figure out what you want (and don't want), the faster you can set about to get there. Your wife will be happier too.

Golfer Nick Price once said, about his marriage troubles, "We were happily married for eight months. Unfortunately, we were married for four-and-a-half years." Why waste these precious years? Speaking to your troubles, in order to enhance your relationship you must first be certain she is very important to you. What follows is a series of exercises designed to help you understand your level of commitment and interest in your relationship.

> **POINT**
> Deciding what you want and showing it is very attractive

EXERCISE
What would you give up to stay with your partner?

Here is a list of simple questions without simple answers. They may help you to understand where she fits on your private priority scale. You need to think hard about them, as giving up basketball or football forever is a major commitment. The answers are for you only, so be sure to answer truthfully.

- What activities would you choose to give up (permanently) for her (e.g., your favorite sport, fishing, or hunting)?
- Would you quit your well-paying and challenging job and move into one that pays less but has shorter hours so that you could devote more time to your wife, marriage and family?
- Would you cut down on your drinking, smoking or drug-taking, or quit completely?
- How about downsizing your SUV into a cheaper car so you could have more money and not have to work so much, perhaps spend a little more time around the house?

- How about getting rid of that old beater in the garage you've been fixing up for years?
- What are your priorities?

These can be tough questions. And while no one would ever suggest you sacrifice everything for your relationship, it's important for you to get a handle on where your wife fits into your priorities. The burning issue is how important this person is to you and how much you would change your life to keep her. Only you can answer that. If your marriage is in trouble, then one possibility is that you have little or no desire to fix it. Is this true? You know the answer; be honest with yourself.

EXERCISE

What do you like about your wife?

_____

_____

_____

_____

_____

_____

What bugs you about her? (You don't have to fill in every blank!)

_____

_____

_____

_____

_____

_____

The exercise on the previous page is designed to help you begin to surface your true feelings about her and what you really want. Once you become clearer about that, and presuming you decide you're willing to put in the effort to make the relationship better, that attitude will show through almost immediately in everyday life. On a subconscious level, she may already begin to perceive a change.

Conversely, if you aren't keen on staying with her that will show through as well — and likely already has. In fact, that's probably why you're having troubles now. Since you're not willing to make the changes — and you may have good reasons — you need to get prepared for the inevitable end. If you accept the basic premise that co-existing in a bad relationship is not a viable option, you now have two choices: make it better or move toward separation.

Sadly, serial monogamy (a series of relationships or marriages with successive women throughout your life) may be the way of the future for some in the post-John Wayne Era period. We might call this the Larry King Era; in my view it's not the best choice. Perhaps you do too, and that's why you've decided to read this book.

EXERCISE
What is your ideal woman and wife?
Everyone carries within them a model or picture of the ideal man or woman — "ideal," of course, meaning a unique and subjective view that varies from person to person. These are often based on our parents, who dominate our lives during our early years when we are forming our "worldview." The contradictions

and accommodations you form between your ideal self (what you ought to be like), what your parents were like, and who you really are play an important role in how you live your life.

Similarly, your vision of an ideal woman may be based on a combination of your mother's attributes, what your father valued in a woman, and how you adopted or refined the influences of your parents during your life experience. How does your wife stack up to this picture? This is very important. One question to ask is whether you still respect her even though she may vary greatly from your ideal. This exercise will help you develop an answer.

Define what the ideal man and woman would look like to you (i.e., looks, smarts, sense of humor, body type, temperament, hobbies). This is your starting point.

Man	Woman

Describe your father	Describe your mother

Describe yourself	Describe your significant other

How does your partner fit your "significant other" ideal?

What contradictions are there? Are they significant?

Knowing what you want and recommitting your energy to the relationship are vital first steps to showing that you're serious about building a successful relationship team.

CHAPTER 4

Assessing the Players

Your partner

———————————— ✷ ✷ ✷ ————————————

Where is your wife at?

It was Sigmund Freud who confessed after thirty years of psychoanalyzing women that he still did not know what they wanted. They often don't know themselves — or at least not on a conscious level. Just as many a woman has spent time trying to get a read on her man's deepest desires, you've got to take responsibility for understanding your wife better.

After yourself, she's the most important person in your world. Where is she at emotionally and connection-wise with you? You can tell a lot by her actions. Pay attention to what she does, not what she says. In order to determine how to solve your problems, you must first gain a deeper understanding of "where your wife is at" in the relationship. Recognizing and analyzing all the signals and developing a more complete picture of what she wants are critical.

Also, before you undertake any kind of corrective action, you've got to understand women better than you (and most men)

do now. While individual women may differ greatly, the following general rules apply:
- For women, love, and their relationships with you, their friends and their family are an enormous part of who they are and what they value.
- Women need to be loved and cared for in tangible ways. They need to see it, hear it, feel it and know it, plain and simple.
- They need conversation — real communication — in order to build and maintain a love connection with you.
- What you see as nagging or criticism and other negative behaviors may be their reaction to not receiving as much love/attention from you as they need. They could be love-starved.
- Most women's hearts are true, and much of what they do and say to you is reflective of their collective desire to build meaningful relationships.

The elderly woman in the movie *Titanic* said that a woman's heart is as deep and mysterious as the ocean. Men can never possibly know everything about their wife's heart. The upshot is that knowing just a little bit more than the average man will make you stand out. It's worth it to overprepare on this one. It's like that old joke where a bear is chasing two guys in the forest. One guy stops to put on his sneakers. The other guy, curious, asks, "What are you doing that for? You can't outrun a bear." The first one replies, "No, but I only have to outrun you!"

If you're competitive in life, you'll want to be better at relationships than other men, and when you're ready to learn more about your woman's deep ocean of a heart, read Barbara De Angelis's book *What Women Want Men to Know*.

The number one thing you need to consider is that you might not know your wife as well as you think. And even those of you who are saying to yourselves right now, "No way, I know my wife inside out," are probably overestimating your own knowledge. Most men do not know their wives very well — but they believe they do, and that's one reason there's a relationship gap. You need to close it.

What is her current connection level to you?

It is vital you find out your wife's true emotional status within the marriage. It really doesn't matter how much you want to get closer and more romantic; if she's already written you off, it may be too late in the game to save it.

Look objectively at your mate and gather information. First make sure she doesn't have some sort of medical or physical problem (depression, illness) that affects the marriage. If she has psychochemical imbalances, suffers from manic/depressive illnesses or has a serious personality disorder — and the odds of this are slim — this book can only help by recommending you get professional assistance. But if the two of you are relatively average people (as most are) having interpersonal relationship problems, then read on.

You should know at this point that some psychiatrists say that much of all personal unhappiness (depression, addictions, anxiety) stems from problems in close relationships (e.g., marriages). Many conditions being treated medically, with anti-anxiety medicines, anti-depressants and sleeping pills, are actually more psychological than physiological in nature. So although a medical condition may be a convenient scapegoat, remember that it's an unlikely cause of most female distress. The fact is that women act "weird" sometimes because they are starved for love. This book will show you how to begin feeding your wife's need for love and acceptance. Doing your part to make the relationship better could be the best and only medicine the two of you need.

(On the other hand, if she is genuinely medically depressed or otherwise unable to respond to you, often she can tell you she loves you but is "feeling so down." If your wife is having trouble on a medical/health basis, then you must resolve this issue before you can work effectively on your marital troubles. Your family doctor is the first place to start.)

What makes today's women tick

It's pretty clear many women are in conflict. On the one hand, they have the sense of wanting to be independent, strong and in charge. And they have become very good at that. On the other hand, women have a history of millions of years of being controlled, dominated, protected and influenced by the males of the species.

There is one theory that states that, even though women may profess to be independent, and act so, deep down they're genetically programmed to be attracted to confident, strong-willed, no-nonsense men who take charge and can protect them. This is the caveman stereotype. The John Wayne model plays off this, but is out of touch for many of today's women because it is inequitable. One way forward is for twenty-first century man to combine the caveman persona with the modern skills of communicating well and paying attention, treating his partner as an equal, getting along with others and having a sense of humor. In this persona he is much more likely to be attractive to the opposite sex. In other words, you don't have to "change" so much as grow. Work to add some new skills to the mix.

The Internet e-book by David D'Angelo, *Double Your Dating*, elaborates on the new attraction in detail. His main point is that men must be "cocky and funny" and build their personal male power and presence. While you may or may not agree with the author, he outlines what he believes makes women tick and how men can use this information to connect more effectively with the opposite sex. To his credit, he rejects men using his ideas for dishonest or insincere ends. In fact, he believes that getting a better handle on what women really want enables men to be more direct about what they themselves need — food for thought for those who want to improve their understanding of the opposite sex. I bet Sigmund Freud would have learned something from this book.

History is important

Your wife's history is one place to start.

Were her parents happily married or did they fight often and/or divorce? Try as we might not to, we often unconsciously emulate our parents' marriage in our own. They are our role models for our feminine and masculine ideals. We always attempt to create our own unique ideal types, but our parents still dominate our creative thinking. If her parents argued a lot, she might work to avoid any strong disagreements. On the other hand, she may approach conflict offensively and be accustomed to shouting it out to win her point. Either way, she could end up having a similarly styled marriage.

People often choose partners for reasons that can be traced back to their families. They may consciously or unconsciously try to re-create their parents' marriage in their own, or, alternatively, work actively to make it as different from their parents' relationship as possible.

This, by the way, is true for you as well. You need to ask yourself what your parents' marriage was like and how your father interacted with your mother. Their marriage could hold important clues not only about your behavior, but also about your relationship and its future. What was your father like? Angry, argumentative, distant, fun-loving, silent, cruel? The old saying is that the apple doesn't fall far from the tree.

A history of abuse affects everything. If either of you suffered sexual, physical or verbal abuse, this will affect how the two of you relate, and make your relationship much more complicated. Was she "popular" at school or a loner? Does she tend to be self-conscious or assertive in her dealings with others? This information needs to be added into your analysis.

Most men are behind the curve

Since men are already behind the curve from where their women are, the corrective measures they attempt when they realize the relationship is in trouble often serve only to make matters worse. One reason is that many men do not understand or analyze women's comments correctly; instead, they often miss them completely or misinterpret them. Or they react angrily without really taking the time to listen carefully. To further complicate the issue, women may not communicate directly how annoyed and upset they are.

There are very good reasons for this. First, from a million years of human relationships dating back to caveman days, women have learned to tread cautiously around their men. Even today, for some there continues to be the threat of physical violence and verbal abuse. This is not to mention simple human pride and ego, which can keep women from putting themselves in vulnerable positions by speaking bluntly to men. As a result, they often choose to couch their true feelings in vague terms. For instance, they might "trash talk" you back (a situation that may have a fun air of male bonding at the time), which you may take as a sign of closeness — when actually they could be communicating their unhappiness with you. If you're not paying attention, much can slip past you.

Sex, the miners' canary

Years ago, coal miners took a canary with them down into the mines. When poisonous gases emerged, the smaller canaries died first and provided an early warning to the miners that something was wrong. Everyone escaped to safety.

Similarly, most relationship experts agree that the frequency and quality of sex in your relationship is your miners' canary for how well your marriage is doing. By examining her attitudes about and interest in sex with you, you can get a good read on where she is emotionally. This important topic is discussed in detail in Chapter 5 (Assessing the Team). Make no mistake: sex is a key indicator.

Getting in shape

Another indicator could be what kind of shape she's in physically. One friend was working out a lot, regaining her BK (before kids) figure. Women (and guys too) often do this when they're about to go back into the singles market. They want to feel more attractive, and getting back in shape is a big part of it. In this particular case, everyone noticed. A few weeks later, she was ready to tell the world she was leaving him. (Now, it's important to note that exercising more could be driven merely by her wanting to be more healthy. However, these are all signals you need to observe and analyze.)

In this particular case, she had stopped working on solving the marriage's problem and started focusing on herself: working out, going out with the girls, buying new clothes, getting her hair done, etc. If your partner is exhibiting some of these signs, then consciously or otherwise she may have stopped focusing her energies on building the relationship and be working to reclaim her own life.

Here's a question: has she started going out with her friends a lot more? Is she spending more time out of your orbit? Now, independence is a good thing. It's all part of the equality of the sexes that men have supported these last couple of decades. After all, if the guy can go out with *his* friends, why can't she go out with hers? However, when there is a change in how your wife socializes, and it doesn't include you, it can be a red flag. In football scouting terms, there's a "tendency" there. The sign is even more ominous if you're not having sex regularly. If she starts reconnecting with old friends — especially male ones — it's probably third down, or maybe even fourth and long.

Buying new clothes

Another leading indicator is buying stylish new clothes for work or leisure when she hasn't been in the habit of doing this before. Again, when you were closer, clothes might be bought together; but now maybe you're too bored to go shopping with her or perhaps she doesn't invite you along anymore. Are you getting the sense that she may be preparing for something?

Other signals about her state of mind

Subtle but just as telling signs include slight verbal digs at you in front of others, not coming to your rescue when others are trash-talking you, and being more willing to be confrontational with you on many small matters that previously she would let slide. Does it seem as if your credits in her bank have run dry?

Now all these signals by themselves don't say it's over. They are all just little bits of information that contribute to helping you gain a better understanding of your wife's emotional state and connection to you. They are also very important in determining your game plan for resolving your marriage woes.

When you're looking for them, all these behaviors are fairly obvious. They follow less noticeable signals that came before. Although it's a common male belief that women are often illogical, in fact this process is completely logical, as are most women. There is a thread woven through that is plain to see if you are looking at the fabric of your relationship with a critical eye. However, if you don't pay attention within the context of a relationship in crisis, the individual significance of these items may be lost on you. If a number of these signals appear together, they have the potential to add up to trouble.

Right now you may be recognizing some or all of these signals in your own situation and chomping at the bit to bring them up with her.

Stop right there!

You must tread cautiously, as you don't want to give her an opportunity to "crystallize" her opinion on the state of your marriage (more on this in Chapter 5) — and that's just where a confrontation could lead. You likely need more information (scouting) in order to diagnose the situation accurately before acting.

What if she's playing games?

"But what if she's into playing head games?" some of you are wondering. Frankly, this is a remote but not impossible scenario. Or perhaps she's been so emotionally traumatized in her early years that she has serious psychological problems (again, unlikely but possible). In any case, if you think this may be true, read on to learn more about your partner and gauge her true level of interest in the relationship.

TIMEOUT

While attending a marriage seminar on communication, David and his wife listened to the instructor declare, "It is essential that husbands and wives know the things that are important to each other." He addressed David, "Can you describe your wife's favorite flower?" David leaned over, touched his wife's arm gently and whispered, "Pillsbury All-Purpose, isn't it?"

Ouch! With any luck, you know your wife a little better than David. Let's do a little quiz and find out.

EXERCISE
How well do you know your wife?

Answer the following questions (the point becomes much clearer if you do this in writing):

- What is her eye color?
- How many times has she changed her hairstyle in the last two years?
- Is her original hair color now turned to gray?
- How would she describe her hair color exactly?
- What's her favorite color?
- If she decorates, what style does she like?
- Who are her three best friends in order?
- What is her biggest regret in life?
- Name her favorite musical artists and albums.
- Does she like flowers, and if so what kind?
- Who are her role models?
- Name her favorite restaurant and food dish.
- What's her favorite drink?
- What kind of clothes does she like?
- If she could meet anyone, who would it be?
- When was the last time she changed the décor in the kitchen or bathroom?
- Does she like to go dancing?
- What are her hot sex buttons?
- What are her fantasies?
- Does she enjoy doing housework?
- What does she love/hate most about her body?

These questions could go on. If you don't know the answers, you haven't been paying attention; you may not really know your wife as well as you thought. Before you can give her what she wants and needs, you must discover who she really is. Start paying careful attention. Listening more effectively and remembering what you hear would be a great start. I wish I had. I'll pass along some hard-earned tips on how to do that shortly.

CHAPTER 5

Assessing the Team

You as a couple

※ ※ ※

By now you've gained some specific information about your unique relationship. You've also learned a lot more about your inner self and probably your wife as well. At this point you may have a handle on what you want, and a better idea of whether your wife is happy or not. Now you need to take an honest look at your dealings with each other and how you work together in your relationship team, using some leading indicators as a guide.

Communication patterns: yours to choose

Look at your relationship from the outside for a second. How do you and your wife communicate? Are your interactions filled with what Dr. William Glasser describes as "the seven deadly habits of external control psychology": criticizing, blaming, complaining, nagging, threatening, punishing and bribing, or rewarding to control? Do either of you try to manipulate the other's behavior to meet your own needs?

If these habits are present, then you already know what you need to work on. What's interesting to note, however, and Glasser's book *Getting Together and Staying Together* explains it best through a concept called "choice theory," is that you can change only the way *you* choose to think and act; you have no power over your wife's conduct. Ultimately, attempting to influence her behavior is a losing proposition. Ditto for her trying to control you.

> ...little or no sex is an enormous red flag

You choose how to behave in the relationship — and you have the power to choose differently. Many problems occur when one of the partners tries to control/change the other's behavior (called "external control" by Glasser). If you can learn one thing about relationships, let it be this: focus on changing your own relationship skills and behaviors, and leave other people to take care of theirs.

I would also be remiss if I didn't also list the key concepts of Glasser's "seven caring habits of choice theory" as they apply to keeping a relationship thriving:

- Listening (more on this later)
- Supporting
- Encouraging
- Respecting
- Trusting
- Accepting, and
- Always negotiating disagreements

How many of these techniques are you exhibiting day in, day out? Glasser's small book is an invaluable guide to building a successful marriage.

Sex and your relationship

You knew we'd get here. We all know that sex is a mission-critical indicator of where the rubber hits the road in a relationship. The key question: how often it is happening? If the answer is zero or not very often, don't kid yourself; little or no sex is an enormous red flag. Aside from close observation of her demeanor and what she says to you, the best way to get more information from your partner is to pursue sex.

First, if she's agreeable, that's great. But don't pat yourself on the back just yet. It could have a lot more to do with her needs than her emotional connection with you or your prowess in the sack. In any case, you can still benefit from finishing this book and implementing its strategies, as the tips involved will inoculate your relationship against future breakdowns.

On the other hand, if her answer is "no, thanks" — all the time or on a fairly regular basis — you have a serious problem. If sex occurs once in a while but only just, the question becomes a different one. Is it just enough for her to maintain the perception of a marriage or is it truly because you are both too busy? Is there a health problem involved? The answer is critical: you'd better find out.

One positive indicator would be if both of you are talking honestly about sex and really addressing the problem. The hard reality, however, is that if you aren't totally clear on why you're not having sex regularly or her reasons don't seem acceptable to you, then your marriage could be at the "fourth and long" stage.

You may disagree. The way I see it, though, most guys are ready and willing. So if the limiting factor here is your wife's interest level, then you need to know that (with rare exceptions) if a woman does not feel a romantic/emotional connection to a man, there's little chance she'll be a willing partner in bed. And, if there's no connection, then (from your side) there's a strong possibility you aren't doing the right things in your relationship. Troubled territory may lie ahead.

(Before going on, here's one caveat to consider: during the time when babies are coming on the scene, some women experience a significant loss of interest in sex. This could be due to hormonal fluctuations or nursing, but may also be simply a reflection of her exploring her new role as a mother. If you're a new father with young children, be sure to expect a temporary loss of interest and cut your wife some slack in the sex department. After kids come along, life at home gets a lot more complicated and stressful. That reduces one of the essentials for sex — a relaxed, unhurried lifestyle — and so having sex becomes more challenging. Fine, but if more normal patterns haven't resumed within four to six months you may be headed to a place you don't want to go.)

Back to the topic at hand. One guy made the point that he was "okay" with not getting sex, that it was the "price to be paid" for being married with kids. For most women, though, the desire to have sex comes from an emotional attraction and connection with her man. It's fundamental. If she doesn't feel like it, immediate corrective action is required.

So if she's not into having sex with you, it may be time to ask why. As a male, you probably consider sex your right within the relationship. However, you may also be an idiot who doesn't deserve it, and therefore she has a right to say no. Regardless, you deserve to know the truth, even if you don't like the answer; it's better than pretending everything's okay while the best years of your life slip away. This is where things can get dicey. Without question, this could become a painful session, but you need to get more details on how she's feeling so that you can properly evaluate your marriage. You can't let it slide into becoming a non-issue.

If possible, you want to control this particular discussion very carefully so that it's kept at a superficial level that will not blow up into her defining moment of crystallization. Under no circumstances can you allow yourself (or her) to get upset or angry. Your goal here is to get information to take away and analyze.

Preferably, this "why we're not having sex" discussion should take place when you're going to bed, and preferably in the dark so that both of you can concentrate on the words and not each other's physical presence. Plus — rather than talking this delicate subject to death — there can be a reasonably quick ending to the conversation, i.e., you both need your sleep.

Typically, to avoid dealing with the issue until she's ready (and possibly already fully detached from you, by the way), she's probably been passing you the "I've been so tired lately" or "I've got a headache" answers. You must go a bit further, past this first layer of defense.

You need to probe deeper and inquire if there's something she would like to talk about, maybe something you've done to upset her. It could be just a few small items that you can address — like playing basketball only twice a week instead of five times (!), or not going out with your buddies quite so often.

On the other hand, it could be something really big that she's noticed and is reacting to — like her being an environmentalist while you finance oil exploration in national parks. Whatever the problem, you need to become aware of it.

At this point, you must listen very carefully to her answers. You can then choose to confront her immediately — and lead the conversation about her feelings to its inevitable conclusion — or take that information away with you and think about it in detail along with the other clues you've gathered.

I recommend the second strategy; remember, Rome wasn't built in a day, and your relationship could take as long to rescue. Scout for your game plan.

Five stages of marital breakdown

There are several stages in the marriage breakdown process. They could be broken out into five main phases: tolerance, disillusionment, second chance, partial detachment and final detachment. Briefly, they are as follows.

Tolerance of your behavior is just that. She stops complaining/commenting about your going out drinking, playing sports or ignoring the children. This is what could be termed a "phony war," as it appears she is okay with the situation and that everything is fine by her. She probably isn't. Sex at this point is non-existent or she participates with little energy. She may say she's worn out or not feeling sexy.

In the *disillusionment* phase, she becomes even unhappier and resigned to the fact that things will never change. She begins to project today's unhappiness and your poor behavior into the next forty years. She then chooses to pull those four decades of future pain back into her feelings about you today. That's a lot of pain — no wonder she's not as happy as she could be! The result is increasing unhappiness as she piles those future years of grievances upon you. Can you feel the weight? This begins to show in her attitude and behavior around you and others. She gets grumpy. Sex at this point may be very rare.

Second chance. At some point, she sees that this can't go on and may confront you. Or you may notice her coolness, request a second chance and actually shape up for a few months. You enter a quasi-second honeymoon phase before you both fall back into the old patterns. This stage may include counseling that ends without really addressing the problem. Although she may present the image that everything is better, it may not be.

Partial detachment. The next stage is where the point of no return lies. Women begin detaching emotionally from their men and distancing themselves. They criticize more frequently (at least to others) and begin to visualize themselves as being separate from the marriage. During this stage they can lose interest in sex (with you, that is!) permanently as their emotional connection drifts. In addition, they may start working out to get in better shape, and start identifying with their friends more.

> [Many men] live in a fool's paradise

Detachment. In this phase women now see their lives as totally separate from that of their partners; sex is completely out of the question and they want to move on as quickly as possible. They have fully detached and want out. This is often when they first tell you the marriage is over. Ironically, this frequently comes as a complete shock to the man.

The problem for most men is that, under the John Wayne provider model, they can't really imagine her ever leaving the safety of their marriage. Maybe they play a game of chicken, hoping she'll turn away at the last second. Men invariably fool themselves into thinking that things are "not that bad." They live in a fool's paradise. For example, they'll view the more serious partial detachment stage as the less serious tolerance or disillusionment stage: "She's a little upset but she'll be okay if I pull up my socks a little." If they take "the wife" out for dinner and stay home from golf on a Sunday, they figure that's enough.

Unfortunately, these little baby steps often just serve to further infuriate her. Similarly, when women are in the detachment stage men delude themselves that it's not that far along. Yet when women detach emotionally, it's rare they can reattach, even though — because of the kids or other pressures — they may want to. Meanwhile the man is still thinking he'll get to play more golf when she comes to her senses, recovers from her PMS, whatever. Wrong.

In so many cases, the man is way behind the curve. Not surprisingly, he doesn't know, because his wife hasn't crystallized her negative feelings into a public stance that is loud enough to finally register on his radar screen. (Here's where paying attention — an area in which we men are often highly deficient — could save a lot of grief.)

On the upside, the great thing about how she may be pulling back future unhappiness into the present is that this represents an enormous leveraging of the potential pain. A number of sincere changes by

> HOPEFUL MOMENT
> Big upside for you

you today can greatly affect this perception, to the extent that the pain can be deleveraged quite quickly and turned into positive feelings. This, of course, is all predicated on you doing the right things and being "real." More on this later.

Crystallization and going public

Crystallization — what is it? Well, currently (unless it has blown apart already), your marriage may be operating on what's called a "false front" basis, i.e., you and she are presenting a façade to each other (and to friends and relatives) that the marriage is still alive and functioning. In actual fact, the reality for one or both of you may be markedly different. For her, this can swing all over the place over time depending on how she's feeling at a given moment. She's not completely detached from you yet.

However, if at this point you say or do something to get her to tell you the truth, those mere shadows of discontent could be made concrete for her. That is, the current reality for her (which, if you had the skills, time, energy, desire and information, you could work hard to change) can become the "official" state of the marriage as you and she profess it to each other and the world. In a nutshell, once she makes a definitive statement that the relationship is in trouble, on the rocks or over, or that you are a buffoon, that becomes the baseline of where the marriage is from her perspective. She has lost hope. She has gone public.

Once it has been crystallized, it becomes much harder (but not impossible) for her to back down from that public position. The marriage is that much closer to ending. Therefore, your immediate mission, should you choose to accept it — while you try to make the long-term changes necessary to rescue the relationship — is to keep her temporary disillusionment with you from becoming permanent. In short, do not incite her to say things that could crystallize her negative feelings toward you! This last point is very important. Read it over and over again until you're sure you understand it.

> Most importantly: don't confront her!

(If crystallization has already taken place for her, at this stage your last hope may be a "grand gesture." To regain her trust at this fragile time, tiny changes may not suffice. Don't misunderstand: this is not to manipulate her back to you — you need to really mean it! Grand gestures won't sway some women, but if you really want to save the relationship it's worth a shot. Specific examples of grand gestures are discussed later, in the Tips section.)

Just because you believe you communicate well with your wife and that your marriage is unique, don't think you should put this book down right now and ask her about her true feelings for you. First, she will either deny she has a concern outright, or explode with her true state (as she knows it at the time) and crystallize her unhappiness. If you're truly interested in saving your marriage, analyze everything first, plot strategy and then move forward. Don't let her on the inside just yet. Finish your research. Skip no steps. Most importantly, DON'T CONFRONT HER!

Don't make the common mistake of thinking you have a unique marriage that is the exception to the rule, as you may let yourself in for a surprise. In rescuing your marriage, your wife must be considered your target and not your confidante.

Only when you have rebuilt her commitment to the marriage can you begin confiding in her again as "us."

EXERCISE
What is the public face of your marriage?
Answer the following questions:
- Do the two of you present the image of a happy marriage to the outside world while there are serious problems within it?
- Has the relationship broken down so badly that you openly argue, she rolls her eyes when you speak, and neither of you backs down?
- Would it be a surprise to most of your friends and family if the marriage ended?

Fit your answers into your relationship analysis.

Love and lust

The word "love" is used so freely today that its meaning has become obscured. Most often, it's wrongly confused with lust and sex, and that one confusion has to be responsible for more relationship troubles in modern society than any other error. Here's an overview of love versus lust.

Lust is that early phase of a relationship in which the two of you have a powerful physical attraction. The sex comes easily and often. This physical attraction is so powerful that it's hard to believe it will ever end — but it does; experience tells us this is so.

Eventually, as the psychologists say, your ego boundaries snap back into normal position. (In guy talk, this means you decide you should have a life away from her and that your impending tee time beckons. You need to connect with your pals and the world away from her in a round of golf or some other activity.)

When the lust/ego phase does scale back, what is left between the two of you determines whether the relationship will continue or falter. Matchmakers say that opposites attract, but that people who are similar often enjoy a deeper, more lasting relationship.

The problem for many people is that a powerful sexual attraction (whether of opposites or likes) can paper over the differences between a man and woman for years during the courting phase — often resulting in marriage, when parting company would have been wiser. The point is, don't confuse short-term lust and sexual attraction with love. But how does one know the difference?

Lust, of course, we understand: it's that animal attraction. Let's consider a simple definition of love (the more important of the two).

Love is the almost unconditional caring for another person, animal or thing. In interpersonal relationships, it involves giving without expecting anything in return.

Take your best buddy as an example. Imagine a scenario in which you know what your buddy wants and needs (beer, game tickets, good car parts, etc.) and you want to help him get it, even without being asked. Although the friendship is often superficial and may include lots of trash-talking and pranks, the mutual regard is real. Besides the doing-things-together connection, it just feels comfortable.

Naturally, there are different levels of love. We can't confuse love for pals or motorcycles or golf with the kind of love that exists between you and your family, you and your children and, most importantly, you and your wife. Not to get too deep about it, but, in its proper form, the spiritual love connection that comes with a true romantic, intellectual and physical connection with your wife is special and unique. It's intimacy, and it's sacred. Whether your dad showed you how important intimacy is or not, we all strive for love; sadly, many don't get it — or worse, don't know what it is when they do get it.

For women, love and relationships are central to their cores, whereas for men they are just one aspect of life. This doesn't mean that once she "loves" you, you're in. Today, quite the opposite is true: love is so important to women that if you trifle with it it'll be "game over." Read De Angelis to get a deeper understanding of just how significant relationships and love are to women, and why you need to upgrade your skills in this area.

> QUESTION
> Do you feel more "comfortable" with your buddies than your wife? If so, is that because you don't have the know-how to make your relationship with your spouse work well, or because you simply don't have the desire to make it work?

To understand more about the topic of love and how it's confused in modern society, read *The Road Less Traveled* by M. Scott Peck. It's an in-depth study that gives a good understanding of how people (women especially because they lead the relationship, but men too) confuse love and lust, and how that affects relationships.

What if she's having an affair?

First, get the facts and confirm the truth as best you can. Be sure it is an affair and not just a series of unlikely coincidences that add up to nothing. In one sense, whether she is having an affair or not should not dissuade you getting your relationship-building skills in order. You are still going to have to upgrade those; it just may turn out that she is not the long-term beneficiary of your improvements.

Second, forgetting about the affair for a minute, determine your level of "want to" as discussed in Chapter 2. How much do you really want to stay with her? If the answer is "not much," then the affair may be your getaway vehicle out of a dying relationship. You might even thank her eventually — she's saved you the work of trying to resurrect a mortally wounded relationship.

However, assuming you want to rebuild the partnership and stay with her, keep the following points in mind: everybody makes mistakes and everyone deserves a second chance. Perhaps she's having an affair because she's bored, or because you aren't giving her the quality, focused attention she needs. There could be many reasons — and some of them could be your fault. Consider what these may be, and try to determine her level of interest in saving the marriage.

Here's one possibility: you could ignore the affair for a while and continue upgrading your relationship skills to see if it has any impact on her. Remember, however, that at some point you must deal with the problem. Open communication about mistakes is usually the way to go. If you choose to ignore the affair for a period of time, it may be the level of motivation on both sides that's the determining factor in whether or not your relationship survives.

If she's clearly moved on for good, then it's time for you to cut your losses and move on as well. Read on and try your best not to let the negativity from this experience prevent you from seeking a quality relationship.

Feelings flow from thoughts: we choose our emotions

There is a serious misconception operating in our society: the belief that our emotions create our thoughts. By that definition, we are powerless to control our emotions (anger, sadness, etc.), and hence our thoughts, and this widely accepted view has been the justification for all manner of abuse and needless grief. The truth is that human beings generate their own emotions from their thoughts. No matter what a person may believe they feel "in their heart," those feelings really emanate from their heads and the thoughts they choose to think moment by moment. These thoughts emerge from the interaction of events and people in combination with previous experiences (good or bad) and the worldview (perhaps an ideal man/woman model) they have adopted.

EXERCISE

Imagine a scenario in which you have reason to be suspicious your partner is seeing someone else. All the signs are there; the conclusion appears utterly logical. Note the emotions (anger, fear, etc.) you feel as a result of thinking these thoughts. Now, imagine that her secretive behavior can be explained by the fact that she's planning a surprise party for your upcoming birthday. Suddenly her actions seem completely innocent and loving.

As your thoughts change, notice how your emotional state relaxes. Most importantly, note that your anger does not precede your thoughts; your thoughts lead directly to the anger or anxiety you experience. You choose the thoughts to think, which triggers an emotional response — *not* the other way around.

Anger, losing your temper and yelling are choices

The point is that we all choose our emotions and feelings. We cannot evade this responsibility — although some guys might throw their hands up and say that it's out of their control, i.e., "I just lost it." Nonsense. We choose to be angry or jealous, frightened or enraged. Your partner's emotional reactions can tell you much about what she is thinking, as can your anger. Emotional outbursts, for instance, can be a window into a person's thought processes and/or neuroses. Look through the window and you may be surprised at what you can learn, both about her and about yourself.

Before we move on to enhancing your partnership, complete the following exercise. It will help you to crystallize *your* feelings about the true state of the relationship.

EXERCISE
Love versus respect in your relationship

Answer the following questions:

Do you love your wife? If so, give a few specific examples why.

_____

_____

_____

_____

Do you respect your wife? If so, list a few reasons.

_____

_____

_____

_____

Does she love you? If yes, list the reasons as you perceive them.

_____

_____

_____

_____

Does she respect you? How do you know?

_____

_____

_____

_____

Now, turn the page…

To evaluate this exercise, the first thing you must do is discard the love answers. Love is too emotionally charged to reveal true insight into your feelings toward each other. While love is essential, it is respect that is the true foundation of a strong and lasting relationship. Look at those answers. Do they show that you have deep, positive feelings for her? What do they say about her feelings for you? Do you really respect your wife? Incorporate this into your analysis.

(By the way, when I first took this test, my answer was that I had a lot of respect for her. That has been a key factor in having a separation that hasn't been too hard on the children.)

EXERCISE
Improving the love–respect quotient

What things can you do to make your wife feel more loved and respected?

_____

_____

_____

_____

_____

What could your wife do to show more love and respect to you?

_____

_____

_____

_____

_____

Happiness evaluation

Think back to a time when you were really happy in your relationship (for a period that lasted a number of months, not just weeks). In many marriages, this period occurs before the children arrive. During this time, what kinds of things did you do together that made both you and your wife happy? List some of these items and consider resurrecting them once in a while:

_____

_____

_____

_____

_____

_____

Identify some things you miss from those previous happy times. Taking an educated guess, I've made a start for you.

Sex
_____
Possibility of more sex
_____

_____

_____

_____

_____

Patterns of relating

List the areas in which you and your partner are strong as a couple:

_____

_____

_____

_____

_____

List some of the things that may be dragging the relationship down:

_____

_____

_____

_____

_____

Evaluating your compatibility with your partner

Renowned psychiatrist Dr. William Glasser has created a simple but powerful guide to determining your dominant relationship needs and how they match up with your spouse's, using a numerical rating system. A comparison of test scores provides a quick idea of your basic compatibility and the relationship's strengths and weaknesses, as well as your chances for long-term success.

The needs, in order, are survival, love and belonging, power, freedom and fun.

- Survival: are you a risk-taker (low survival need) or very careful (high)?
- Love and belonging: do you tend to be a loner (low) or do you like to be around other people (high)?
- Power: are you easy-going (low) or do you like to be in charge all the time (high)?
- Freedom: is your life highly structured (low) or do you enjoy spontaneity (high)?
- Fun: do you like doing things and having fun (high) or is it just not that important to you?

EXERCISE

In this exercise, rate the strength of your needs as described above in each of the five areas on a scale of 1 to 5, with one being very low and five being very high. Compare your overall score with that of your spouse.

	Your score	Your partner's
Survival		
Love and belonging		
Power		
Freedom		
Fun		

Glasser's analysis of the results is valuable and too detailed for this section (I recommend reading *Getting Together and Staying Together*). However, his main point is that a difference of two points or more between spouses on a particular need is of some concern. One or two gaps of this magnitude may be overcome provided the partners can negotiate the difference. In his opinion, a gap of two or more points in a number of the five primary need areas is strongly indicative of a relationship that could get into trouble.

CHAPTER 6

It's Third and Long

Time to get serious

─────────── ✳ ✳ ✳ ───────────

By now, you've read enough to gain a clearer sense of whether you want to keep the marriage together and build a stronger "team." You should also have a much better understanding of where your wife is at, the weak areas of your relationship skills, and the shape your team is in.

Assuming you've consciously decided you want to rebuild and enhance your relationship and have surfaced those feelings during the first few chapters, what happens next is that you start behaving in a manner that automatically begins to reveal your love and regard for her. Also, you've probably begun to consider how you can demonstrate that love in ways that are concrete *from her viewpoint* (see Chapter 7) so that you can get ahead of the curve.

At this point, you also probably recognize that this is very serious business. It's time to make some quality plays and dig your relationship out of its hole. It's definitely third and long.

Now, "third and long" is just a metaphor for how much trouble your relationship may or may not be in. For some who are just starting out in marriage, it could be early in the game, with success or failure a long way from being decided. For others, it could be the end of the fourth quarter, down a touchdown and time for a last-ditch Doug Flutie "Hail Mary" (in relationship terms known as the "grand gesture"). Somewhere in between these extremes are most of us, with the game still up in the air. Our efforts can make a difference.

One of the biggest mistakes I made was in loving my wife the way I thought she should be loved, rather than how she needed to be loved (for instance, I believed that my hard work to keep the lawn looking good would be interpreted by her as loving. It's not that she disapproved of my efforts here, it's just that they didn't speak to her in any special way — in her view it was merely another household chore). Don't make that error.

Go over your analysis and game preparation, carefully understand what your wife needs and wants, then select the plays and skills from the following chapters that will help you demonstrate your commitment in ways that will have a positive and perhaps profound impact on her. While it may sound contrived, it's not: it's giving someone you love the things that will help them feel nurtured in your relationship. It's good "manipulation" — and it can be a man's winning strategy in the marriage game.

CHAPTER 7

Where do we go from here?

Start with the fundamentals

※ ※ ※

The dawning of "Okay, now I realize there's a problem. What should I do to fix it?" is the point at which many men fall down. Often as not, their efforts at making their wife understand they do love her can backfire and cause further trouble, simply because they do not truly understand how she wants to be loved. At this point, the situation is often precarious, with little margin for error. You need some good plays *right now*, improvements that are likely to have strong meaning for her. The next two sections provide a selection of tips you can draw from to show her how much you care. This first section focuses on the fundamentals of a relationship, which, as in sports, provide the foundation for success.

First and foremost: what kind of love does she want?

One of the biggest missteps in troubled relationships comes from giving your significant other love in a form that she (or he) does not want or recognize as loving. If you care about someone, part of the commitment involved is in finding out how they want to be loved, and then working to love them in that manner.

According to Dr. Gary Chapman in his best-selling book *The Five Love Languages: How to Express Heartfelt Commitment to Your Mate*, there are five basic kinds of love for both men and women. Read Chapman's book and see if you can spot the language of love that appeals most to you, and that which you think appeals to your mate. These are what Chapman calls the "primary" love languages. If you're like me, you may kick yourself after reading this, but you'll gain great insight into how to communicate effectively with your partner. If you can't identify her love language, don't panic. Instead, recognize the huge upside: this is an important area that you can target for immediate improvement. Here's a brief summary.

THE FIVE LOVE LANGUAGES
Words of affirmation

A sincere compliment on something she has done well or is wearing is the way forward here. It's called *positive reinforcement* and is one way to get someone to do something of their own free will. In coaching a team of seven-year-olds in soccer, we get them to improve by consistently commenting on the things they are doing right. Everybody loves a compliment, and it is said that credit is something that, given freely, comes back many times over. Your wife may crave words of affirmation.

Here's an analogy that may reveal what's working against you. A sports study asked coaches to identify what percentage of their feedback to their athletes was positive versus negative.

The coaches maintained that it was 90% positive, but close investigation revealed that only 50% of the comments were supportive.

The point is, are you really positive with your wife most of the time or has your relationship become poisoned by negativity? This situation is bad enough, but it could be made much worse if words of affirmation are your wife's primary love language. If you're being negative in your marriage, stop it immediately. Look on the bright side. There is a silver lining to be found in every situation, e.g., "Sure you ran over my favorite golf clubs, but the car needed a new back tire anyhow." On the other hand, she may have run over your clubs deliberately as a way to let you know you're spending too much time on the golf course; either way, there's something positive to be taken out of almost every situation.

Quality time

Quality time is characterized as time spent together by choice, not by force. As Chapman explains, "A central aspect of quality time is togetherness. I do not mean proximity...togetherness has to do with focused attention." A woman who values quality time does not want to feel she is "number one in your heart but number ten on your program" as one friend says. Offering her your time freely and often is the best way to meet her needs for love.

Quality time encompasses both conversation and activities. Another aspect is self-disclosure. When it comes to communication, you can't just listen (important as that is), you must contribute. Always add some personal notes or revelation to make this "quality time."

Receiving gifts

Gifts may be an important symbol of love for your wife, and if so you need to pick up on your gift-giving activities. And no, it's not just buying flowers on Hallmark holidays like Valentine's Day or Mother's Day. You have to be more creative. Look around her world and find things she likes. Does she have a favorite flower (not flour!), or does she tend to buy candles frequently? Bringing home simple little things could be just the way to her heart. If she collects things, this is the perfect avenue for giving gifts. Check the Tips section for specific gift ideas.

Acts of service

Acts of service means that your wife loves it when you do things for her. This could include tidying the house, cooking a romantic dinner, shampooing the carpets, changing the baby's diaper or doing the laundry. Perhaps you could spontaneously bring home fresh seasonal fruit, saving her a trip to the grocery store (this combines gift-giving with acts of service in a very effective way). At any rate, all are acts of love if performed in a positive spirit. It's doing things you know your spouse will really appreciate.

(Note: This does *not* mean doing things that are already in your bailiwick, like mowing the lawn or putting out the trash; it means picking up on a duty that would normally fall to her. Key point on service: remember, you're not doing her a favor by helping her out, you're just pulling your weight! It also has to be frequent and consistent, beyond what is expected. If it's just being done so you can go out with the boys, it won't count in her book. Also, don't tie this to a reward — like sex that night — or she'll be on to your game.)

Physical touch

For many people, touching — often in a non-sexual way, such as holding hands or linking arms — is the language of love that reaches them best. For others, it is less so but still hugely important. Sex is part of this, but often the non-sexual touching is far more critical. Are you forgetting to hug your wife and hold hands often? How about kissing her good night *every* night?

You must learn to communicate to your wife in her primary love language, and that means figuring out what it is. It is urgent you discover this as soon as possible. Read Chapman's illuminating book to learn more.

EXERCISE

What kind of love does your partner want? List the top two, in your opinion:

_____

_____

EXERCISE

What kind of love do you want? List your top two picks:

_____

_____

Over time, use the different love languages with her and observe her reaction very closely. You should be able to tell what reaches her the best. Maybe something as simple as you spontaneously taking the kids off her hands will let her know. Once you get some concrete information, don't forget it: write it down in the Notes section at the back of this book. Read Chapman's book to help reinforce and expand your understanding of this important facet of your relationship.

Keeping her romantically interested

As mentioned earlier, David D'Angelo (*Double your Dating*) believes that women profess to like one type of man — nice, stable, predictable guys — but are actually more attracted to a completely different type — guys who are confident, mysterious, cocky and funny. He believes those attributes are all attraction skills that men can learn in order to build and hold a woman's interest. But, let's face it, it's hard to be mysterious when your wife sees you in your underwear all the time, unshaven, hung over, etc., and knows most of your secrets. She has more inside dirt on you than anyone knows — or would want to know!

Following D'Angelo's thinking, you need to combine the family requirement for predictability and routine with working hard at being spontaneous, surprising and funny. Never stop refining your attraction skills and techniques as you practice them on your wife and others. Within that little confined box called marriage in which you exist, you must be creative and find ways to generate excitement and maintain attraction. We'll outline some ideas later on how to do that. What follows is a list of how-tos for improving your relationship skills, starting with the fundamentals.

> ...the greatest aphrodisiac for women is their man listening with his entire body and soul to them.

These essentials include paying attention to your wife (obvious but largely overlooked); owning your own feelings (feelings? what feelings?); injecting humor (the bond of comedy); getting involved with your kids (sounds easy — are you doing it?); and staying fit/grooming yourself (animal magnetism). These tactics are key to every happy union and form the foundation of any game plan designed to build a stronger partnership.

> Learn to catch your mind wandering and bring it back to focus on her

It's not just a matter of starting to implement these strategies right away (although there's no time like the present); read the entire book first — c'mon, it's not that long! — and then brainstorm before devising a schedule of implementation. Go through the items listed below, understand each one, and try to gain a sense of whether any or all of these are lacking in your relationship.

By the way, these skills are valuable in every relationship, even those with your kids, friends and co-workers. Chapter 8 presents a list of other valuable tips you should know.

1. Number one aphrodisiac: Deep listening

This is it —*numero uno* — whether she is your wife, your mistress or a date. One marriage counselor said that the greatest aphrodisiac for women is their man listening with his entire body and soul to them. Noticing and paying attention is nice (and something many men need to do), but deep listening is what's required to build and grow a connection that will stand the test of time.

What does this mean? Well, to truly listen to a woman is to give her 100percent of your attention by being fully present with her. This kind of listening is not just listening with your ears and eyes, but also listening with your heart and soul.

It's been said that "you can listen another's soul into being." All this sounds mystical, but it is true that this kind of connection allows her to experience the deepest part of herself. Funnily enough, responding with words (especially the wrong ones) only breaks the spell of this kind of listening.

> **POINT**
> The goal of talking with her is not to exchange information, but to build connection

Where men fall down is that they listen carefully to their spouse only in the early years, if at all. As the years go along, they begin treating her like the "little woman" or the hired help (John Wayne Era), or pay attention just to the surface rather than fully focus on her deeper concerns. They fail to respect her or pay close attention to what she says. Over time, as she begins to pick up on this inattention, the gap opens a little wider.

Think about it. Not paying attention is incredibly disrespectful. You wouldn't do this to your boss, right? What about your best friend? If you want more from your relationship — more hugs, maybe even just a smile once in a while — start by listening with much more focus and attention. Begin by learning to catch your mind when it wanders and bring it back to her. What do I mean? First, a bit of background.

Most people believe that communication is about projecting out, telling the world what you have to say and how important it is. It's not: you (and everyone else, for that matter) are not that important. Communication involves listening more than talking — some experts say that 90 percent of your energy and effort should revolve around listening. Someone once said "I don't do any learning while I'm talking." That makes a lot of sense in a marriage. Have you learned anything new about your wife lately?

True listening involves building connection by engaging the other person through the deepest part of them. In your relationship, that means *being silent* and *paying attention* when your partner is talking. Facing her with a relaxed, fully engaged attitude that says to her "you have my undivided attention" is critical. When it's your turn to speak, *show empathy* (that you understand what she's feeling) and, where appropriate, *reflect the feelings* she is talking about back to her to show you understand (be careful here: you don't want her to think you're a parrot, or mocking her). During this entire process, your body language must convey the message *I'm paying complete attention to you and I respect what you have to say.*

RULES FOR DEEP LISTENING
Be silent
Pay close attention
Show empathy
Reflect feelings
Build connection

Women are very subtle communicators. Body-and-soul language is important. Over the hundreds of thousands of years they've had to live with aggressive warrior males, they've learned to be indirect. To understand what they're really feeling, you must seek out the underlying signals. That means paying exceptionally close attention and perceiving her with all your senses. The reason is quite simple: much of communication is non-verbal, occurring through body language and projections. If you pay attention using only your ears and eyes, you won't pick up those signals.

Think you can't do it? Well, it does sound tough at first; many men are used to louder communication (think heavy metal). But, as you become tuned in and skilled at paying attention to your partner's deeper communications, you can sense (read"feel") most of them like the line of a putt or a linebacker leaning in as he's about to blitz. Read the defense, read a woman, the sensing and intuition skills are similar — it's your level of interest and commitment that determine success, both in football and in your relationship.

One key starting point here is to look her in the eye when she talks to you. Check to see if you do this often enough. There's a subtle point here where you must have enough eye contact to let her know you're really listening to her, but not so much that she feels suspicious and wonders what you're doing. (It's also important to remember here that some of the best listening can often occur without eye contact — in the dark, for example — just through focused attention. However, if your relationship has been troubled by the fact that you have been ignoring your wife on a regular basis, she may view your averting your eyes as inattention. She may assume — correctly or incorrectly — that you're daydreaming about your baseball pool.

Be sure to face her and eliminate other distractions. Focus on what she's saying. In other words, don't think you can listen to her while watching TV! Turn the TV off or put the paper down. Maybe you're sure you can do both, but the signal you're sending is that she's worthy of only half your attention. Instead, send the message that she's important to you.

Another essential is to listen actively to her. Pay real attention to what your partner is saying. What emotion messages is she sending out? If she's repeating something she's already told you, don't tune out. Instead, try to figure out why she's doing that. Is it because you didn't really hear her before? Maybe it's because she just enjoys talking/yelling at you. Or is this an ingrained a habit of hers due to your continual habit of semi-attention? You need to understand the difference, pick up the clues and learn. If your inattention has been creating or exacerbating the problem, some focused time spent on correcting this habit could deliver impressive long-lasting results very quickly.

One strategy women sometimes employ, especially if you tend to shoot off your mouth too quickly, be dismissive of ideas, or be a hot-headed caveman type, is to spend a little time warming you up with conversation before hitting you with their big point. Be ready for it. When it comes, don't dismiss it or get angry. Your job is to show empathy and reflect feelings, not to overreact or breeze by it. Surprise her with deep listening skills that confirm you are actually paying attention to everything she is communicating.

Moving on, you've all heard about the classic male mistake: trying to solve her problems for her. Don't do this! What she's looking for in a conversation is your interest, understanding — and, most importantly, connection — not your "expertise." This mistake occurs so often that I recommend adopting the phrase "don't solve her problems, just listen" as your slogan; major points if you can remember this one. (Of course, since we, as men, are genetically and culturally programmed to solve problems, a tradeoff here might be to solve her problem in your head but keep it to yourself. See, I've been there.)

Final point. We've mentioned that credit is the something that, once given away, comes back in spades. Paying attention should be put in that same category: If you practice deep listening on your spouse and master it as a skill, you won't believe how much attention you'll get back! In fact, there is no amount of work you can do in the marriage to make it a 50/50 workload. Most women will be so happy with your early efforts in attention-giving that they will automatically start doing more, and so will likely always end up exceeding your contribution. It's simply the nature of the sexes.

The key message is this: listening with body and soul is the number one way to connect with your partner's needs and values. In fact, whether she knows it or not, it's one of the things she's most attracted to, and as such it delivers an enormous payoff for you. As part of enhancing your relationship, you may want to take notes to keep track of what's important to her. Assuming you succeed in staying together, you'll lay the foundation for being a much more involved husband.

(Advanced reading: the *Mars and Venus* series by John Gray is a good place to start on understanding the very real differences between the sexes in terms of communication, as is the De Angelis book.)

DRILL

You need to burn into your memory bank that your job is to practice deep listening! Now, write out 100 times (if you need to): *My job is not to solve her problems, but only to deep-listen.*

2. Own your own feelings: women are tired of the burden

Men tend to be connected to external events and items. Football, hockey, sports, current events, war, card games, work; the list goes on. We're so trained to focus on a limited number of external things that we haven't been educated in spending time on internal values, feelings and relationships — the stuff that most women really care about.

Sadly, often men don't know how they feel about the kids, the wallpaper, Grandma or their wife's new hairstyle, mainly because they don't connect with themselves deeply enough to know how they really feel — about anything. The result is often apathy in the marriage: "Oh, honey, you pick something and I'll be fine with it." (Yep, guilty.) This kind of answer drives women crazy.

The fact is that men are results-oriented — *let's get the job done* — while women are process-oriented, needing to work through things and discuss them fully before moving forward. However, if you don't know how you feel about something, then of course you won't want to discuss it (i.e., better to keep her wondering than open your mouth and confirm for her that you are clueless and/or disinterested!).

But, seriously, since emotions flow from thoughts (as discussed earlier), then identifying your feelings is not that difficult if you can isolate the thoughts you have about the events and people in your life.

Many of the exercises in this book are designed to help you get a handle on how you really feel about your wife, your life, kids, job, parents, etc., and what you want. For many men who grew up with a father who didn't talk about those things, uncovering their feelings is the toughest — but also the most rewarding — step in tilting their relationship toward greater happiness. At the very least, it can help men to become more sure about what they want. Believe me, moving even a little bit closer to knowing what you want will show through in your relationship in a big way by maintaining your personal power. That's something your wife will respect and absolutely love.

3. Inject a little humor into your life

Nothing spoils a romance so much as a sense of humor in a woman — or the want of it in a man.

— Oscar Wilde

Are you a sourpuss who can't take a joke and hasn't had a good belly laugh in years? When was the last time you did something goofy and impromptu with your wife that caused you both to laugh? A good sense of humor is what women often crave most in their mates. Women love to laugh and they're always joking with their friends. If you shy away from humor, especially jokes or comments that involve laughing at yourself, it could be another nail in your coffin.

Let's face it, married life can be a grind at times. It's easy to get in the habit of not having fun and just getting through. Before you know it, years can go by and your outlook on life has changed for the worse.

Has life so soured you that you can't remember the last time you laughed so hard you cried? And if you do laugh once in a while, is it around your wife? Start injecting a little humor into your life by watching a few romantic comedies together, or stand-up comedians live or on TV. You could also get your funniest friends to come over more often. Quit being negative and work on having fun and seeing the positive side of life. Comedy can be a real bond. The woman you want to impress will love this (so will your wife — ha ha). As one woman mentioned on an online service: "Humor is so important that without it you are just some stuffy, uptight, boring guy waiting to have a heart attack." It wouldn't hurt to put a little effort into bringing humor into your partner's life.

4. Pay attention to the junior members of the team

"Once we had a baby he was involved for the first little while," said Alecia, one friend who separated from her husband. "Then he got bored with the routine and only played the doting dad when the family came over and it was showtime. I was left with getting up in the middle of the night while he lived the life of Reilly. Does that sound fair?"

There's little doubt that relationships frequently go off the rails when children come onto the scene. A number of things happen that make it harder to keep your relationship positive and healthy. First, your wife is harried from taking care of infants. She may still be overweight from carrying your child and feeling a little frumpy and/or down. Plus, maybe her hormones are acting up, making her susceptible to mood swings she didn't seem to have before. Unfortunately, you can't nurse the baby and may feel unqualified to help in other areas, so she ends up doing the lion's share of the work. Ironically, while she's in "overwhelm" mode, you're getting a little bored.

At this point, it's hard not to think, "Well, I'll just turn on the TV and keep an eye on the game." At this point, combined with your parents' style of your mom taking care of the kids while dad watched TV or played golf, you are about to fall into the trap of "not pulling your weight with the kids." This is how resentment starts and begins building, leading to reduced connection and an emerging relationship gap that, left unchecked, can lead eventually to detachment, separation and divorce.

Becoming parents, especially after the second child, alters a couple's relationship forever — for better or worse — and unfortunately many couples are not prepared for the changes.

You can avoid this trap, however. Here's how: get involved with the kids right away and stay involved; be overtly and overly helpful to your wife in child-care matters. (If you are not prepared to do this, you might want to reconsider whether you are ready to be a father.) Don't make the mistake of thinking she has everything handled and you might as well go to the bar and have a beer.

Remember that your wife has a head start here: her nurturing instinct has been activated by childbirth. But make no mistake: she's watching to see how well you rise to the occasion. You need to continue being "male" — that's vital to her attraction for you — but when kids are involved, you have to tap into your nurturing side (you do have one). This is just the way it is when the family workload increases. You must pull your weight if you want to keep your family together for the long haul.

One possible way forward here — I wish I'd done this — is to let her get a little sick of you. Consider doing twice what you think is needed. Be so helpful — "fake it 'til you make it" — that you begin to enjoy the work. She just may decide to thank you for your efforts. Let her tell you to get out of the house, go play golf, or drink beer with your friends in the garage. Women do cut men some slack in this regard if they can see a concerted effort. The danger zone is if she urges you to go but is really testing your sincerity — this is distinctly possible if your involvement to date has been less than stellar. This can be a minefield, especially early postpartum when she may be highly emotional. Get to know her subtle signals. Again, listen to her body language: what she does, not what she says. And use common sense. If it looks like there's a lot to be done, start to do it; don't wait to be asked. Doing the right thing, right away, is a winning play. Isn't this one of those things we were all supposed to learn in kindergarten?

When you *are* around, she will also be noticing whether you are there in spirit or just in body. When you're with your kids, really be there. Make it quality time as much as possible. You'll enjoy your time with and without them even more if you do this. Learning how to show this type of commitment and attention — and really mean it — will tell her much about where she and the children are situated on your priority list.

> POINT
> Why is it that a man can easily play 36 holes of golf but is too tired to walk around the block with his wife?

5. Get in shape

The reason is obvious: Pillsbury doughboys are not attractive. Flimsy excuses like "just more of me to love" and "I could lose it if I wanted to" don't cut it these days. If you look better you feel better, and that increases your attractiveness to the opposite sex.

Bonus: if you're fit, you'll have a better sex life. Is that good, or what?

I'm not saying that you have to be buff like Arnold Schwarzenegger. Just get your body fat down to a reasonable level. Lose that extra fat (men can do this much more easily than women because they have significantly more muscle mass to help burn the fat). Start working out more. Adopt a muscle-building, weight-lifting, calorie-reducing program. Also, do some cardio work so you won't be running out of gas all the time.

If you haven't worked out in years, don't start running right away, as you might fall victim to a heart attack or a serious injury. Talk with your doctor. He'll probably tell you to just start with walking and build up your distance gradually. You can combine that with a bit of walking/running, and gradually move full-time into running. Walking or running — preferably *with* your wife — is the way to go. Get a good book on basic fitness, or a personal trainer, to guide you.

You can start walking on your own; build up your distance gradually. When you're ready to move into more physical work, consult your doctor and a fitness consultant at the local gym. The doctor can give the okay, while the fitness consultant can set up a graduated program of exercise.

When you're ready, invite your wife along. She'd have to really hate you to say no. (If she tries to get you to take up hard running right off the bat, though, be suspicious, especially if she's just increased your life insurance policy!)

6. Groom yourself, cave man

Nose hairs sticking out, the unshaven look, dandruff, butt "cleavage," shaggy hair, dirty fingernails, b.o., bad breath, scummy teeth: they're are all turnoffs for your wife — er, for most women, anyway. Take care of these things. Shave when you know you're going to kiss your wife. Looking scruffy works only if you're a twenty-something rock star and the look is deliberate. Other strategies can be effective for the guy who knows what he's doing and has style.

Don't know what to do in this area? Get your sister or a good friend (male or female) to give you advice. Seek out people whose style you admire. Here are a few basics.

In clothes you don't have to have high style (although it couldn't hurt), but these days men definitely have to be presentable. This means color-coordinated choices that suit you, fit comfortably, and are clean and well maintained. You don't need to be reminded (or do you?) that fresh underwear and socks each day are essential. In other words, shower and change even if your favorite team is on a winning streak and you're worried about bad karma. One more thing: please don't ever wear socks with sandals!

EXERCISE
Deep breathing

It may sound a bit hokey but stay with me on this one. Ever notice on TV when NBA players like Steve Nash take a deep breath at the line before shooting a foul shot? Football players do the same thing on the field. Wasn't it Jerry Rice who was promoting those Breath-right nose bandages to improve air flow?

Deep breathing helps pro athletes connect their minds and bodies to perform more effectively. It's the same in your marriage. When you're having trouble figuring something out, making a decision, or determining how you really feel about something, take a long, slow, deep breath, hold it briefly and then let it out gradually. This is a simplified form of meditation used by many high-performance athletes. And it may help you to stop being so reactionary.

Meditation is another way to help speed the process of discovering your true feelings in life. Pro athletes have also found it incredibly helpful in improving their sports performance. Why not aim to reach Jerry Rice's level of skill in your marriage?

CHAPTER 8

Your Relationship Playbook

More tips and techniques

※ ※ ※

In addition to the fundamental strategies laid out in the last chapter, there are a variety of additional tips and techniques that can help you expand your relationship skills and performance. Examine the following items and decide which ones can be of assistance. At the end of the book you'll find exercises designed to help you select the tips you need to implement, and determine the order in which they should fall within your relationship game plan.

The number one point is not to pick tips that you think will "work" on your wife. It's to select those that you *truly believe* are needed to improve your relationship. If you've been reading carefully and taking the information to heart, you probably already have a good gut feel about many of the changes you need to make.

Pay attention, there'll be a quiz later

By now you've realized that this relationship stuff requires some work. And also by now you've acquired many of the skills needed to see her signals left, right and center. Her likes and dislikes, how she feels about things, what makes her feel loved — it's all finally showing up on your radar screen. So many signals, how do you track it all?

Once I started dating a woman and we would meet for coffee on a pier. The first time she ordered a "mocha skim milk." The second time we got there, I asked her what she would like. The answer was given a little frostily: "mocha skim milk." I got the message loud and clear that time. The third time, I ordered mocha skim milk for her and could see her noticing that I remembered. I avoided one land mine and scored some points. Small points, mind you, but at the same time — what do they say in sports? — take care of the little things and the big things will take care of themselves.

A similar thing happened when I ran into someone I had once dated. Again, coffee was on the agenda; I casually mentioned her favorite hot drink at Starbucks (white chocolate mocha) and she was impressed that I remembered. I was rather impressed too.

Whether you know it or not, women are testing all the time. How many times has your girlfriend or wife stopped in a store and said, "I like that," and then mentioned it in passing later and been annoyed at your not remembering? Or perhaps she's been more direct: "That would be a great birthday gift, don't you think?" (Okay, if you miss a hint like this one, you *really* need to do some work.) But say you catch the hint, then vow to come back and buy the item a week or two later — and then promptly forget. This happens to men all the time, and is a direct result of — sorry, guys — sheer laziness. You will score major brownie points if you can remember your partner's tastes and incorporate them into your relationship-rebuilding game plan. But how?

Take notes

In my case it tends to be a matter of volume. For example, the mocha skim milk point I remembered. However, when she started talking about her likes and dislikes, it was hard to keep track of all the things that made her unique. What types of movies, foods and drinks she liked, whether she hiked or not (she did), etc. Not to paint us all with the same brush, but, for men, remembering these precious little nuggets can often get lost in the overwhelming complexity and importance of keeping up with work, the weekend baseball scores, or our golf, hockey and [insert your favorite] pools.

In the dating phase, when the attraction is running high, it's easier to remember this stuff. But once that capture phase wears off and you've become a pair, with an accumulation of shared experiences, it's natural to become complacent. As hunters and warriors, men are not programmed to focus on the small details. Note to self: this could become a problem.

Bottom line is, if you're being tested, then school is in session and you have to take notes. It sounds mechanical and contrived to make notes about your loved one's likes and dislikes, but maintaining a relationship can be hard work; taking notes just makes the job a little easier.

Warning: it's best if she does not find your notes, as she may misinterpret the exercise. This is simply meant to be a helper for you while you're learning better memory skills. If you're like me, the act of writing these things down is all that's needed to ensure you remember them. You'll find room to make notes about your partner in the back of this book.

A. THE BIG STUFF

This is the game plan foundation from which all the other tips flow. Using these techniques will help you to connect more effectively with yourself — and more authentically with her.

The "F" word

The one nice thing about sports is that they prove men do have emotions and are not afraid to show them.

— Jane O'Reilly

Let's talk about the really big stuff right upfront, starting with the "F" word: feelings. Many men do not go deep in this area, except when they talk about sports. That's interesting, given that this is such a biggie for women. When asked how they feel, men might be likely to say, "I feel…like a beer." We generally don't pay attention to how we might be feeling at a particular time, except maybe during a game. Many also don't know how to articulate their feelings. Some women have been known to ignite blow-up arguments with their husbands just to get some emotion out of them as a starting point.

We know where this problem comes from: dads who didn't exhibit their feelings, old movies with stoic John Wayne-like characters, and the lurking presence of a small but powerful descriptor: *wimp*. All these have combined to cause boys and men to put their feelings into small boxes with airtight lids. No wonder so many men block out their feelings. Later, we'll talk a little about how you can reclaim your emotions for yourself, your wife and, perhaps most importantly, your children.

Key indicators of whether you're in touch with your feelings: have you recently felt emotional (i.e., like crying) at a movie or because of something touching your kids did? Feelings are important in your relationship, for two reasons:

- So that you can share them with your wife to build connection and spiritual closeness, and
- So that you can learn how you truly feel about her, and make the commitment to take the relationship to the next level.

TIMEOUT: Children and Feelings

There is one other very important reason to take this tip to heart: it is vital you demonstrate feelings to your children to help them learn how to connect with their own emotions. You must take the lead in educating your children, especially your sons, in this area. Boys look to their fathers for clues about how to behave. This is a hard one, but start displaying emotion in front of your boys (and not just in front of a football game); you'll be doing them a big favor. These emotions might include happiness, sadness, joy and even appropriately placed/communicated anger.

As a bonus, if you show emotion in front of your daughters, they'll look for that kind of emotional depth in other men. For both sons and daughters, you can teach them from an early age about feelings by helping them to label and identify their emotions. When my son found out his best friend would be moving, he looked sad. I said, "Aw, you're feeling sad because Ryan is moving away, right?" He nodded. Moms do this a lot. When your kids get older, you'll be glad you did it too.

Back to your wife. The amount of work involved in rebuilding your relationship is so great that you must be confident about how you feel about her. A strong, positive approach will project magically in everything you do. She'll sense it and in turn it will help build her interest in developing a more positive frame of mind and attraction for you. The feedback will do wonders for your efforts to improve your partnership.

EXERCISE
Connecting with your feelings

A notebook will come in handy for this exercise in personal development. The process will take time (perhaps months), so don't expect miracles right away. This is ongoing development, not a quick fix.

(By the way, I'm not attempting to suggest that *all* men are out of touch with how they feel. I do, however, believe it's a widespread reality for the male of the species.)

Anyway, start with your favorite male activities and ask yourself how you feel about them. Take car engine repairs for example. Answer the question, "When I'm working on my car I feel… [fill in the blank]." The missing word could *be powerful, competent, like a man, active, strong, smart, happy, challenged* or any other feeling word. Write your answers down. Do the same with other favored activities such as work, sports, movies, etc.

Then move on to more important matters such as your religion, your children, your wife and your siblings. Identify the word or words that describe your feelings (you should be able to use many different words, not just one). Also, remember that your feelings will change over time. For example, if you and your wife have an argument, your feelings may be negative but write these down anyway — it's important. Over time, you'll gain an overall sense of how you truly feel about the people and activities in your life.

The other point to remember is that other people can't see your true feelings just by looking at your face. You have to work — hard and sometimes awkwardly at first — at expressing those feelings outwardly so they become visible for others to see.

As you've read earlier, it's vital you take ownership of your own emotions. If you're mad at your wife for something, those feelings are yours. Don't project them on her. When she turns down sex, don't think, "She's making me angry." Think, "I'm feeling angry because I can't have sex tonight." Nobody can make you angry except you. Working from your thoughts, you choose to feel angry.

Know what's really important: NFL versus the "home turf"
I used to say that my wife and I shared the decision-making equally. I took care of the important matters, such as choosing who to vote for in the next election; knowing when to cut the grass; coaching the kids' teams; keeping on top of what was happening in the NFL, NBA and NHL; and knowing just the right time to flip the burgers. My wife would then handle the "other" decisions — like where we would live, how many children we would have, and how our kids would be raised. Hmm, at the time that seemed like a pretty good split to me. Ha! Now I know better.

Are you guilty of avoiding the important things in life and focusing on what amounts to sports trivia? I enjoy sports as much as the next guy, but have come to believe they are not a substitute for a true investment in family life. This is not to mention the fact that most regular-season games are meaningless. As Seinfeld once said, with all the player turnover, we're really just "rooting for laundry." My recommendation to those of you who might be sports junkies is this: at least try to save your heavy watching until the playoffs, when the games start to mean something! There is no doubt whatsoever that your wife will welcome your increased attention on the family front — so much so she will probably hand you over to the playoffs willingly just to show her gratitude. Today, that sounds like a better arrangement to me.

Be real with yourself and others

You've likely heard the joke that sincerity's the most important thing; once you can fake that, you've got it made.

This simply doesn't apply in romantic relationships. This book is not intended for those who plan to manipulate their partners to get what they want. The fact is, women will eventually find you out because they are astute observers of behavior. This is especially true once they get into their 30s and 40s. Using this book and its tips for improving your relationship to "fool your wife" will only buy you a few extra years at best before she wises up.

There's the well-publicized case of the army officer stationed overseas who used the Internet to have email relationships with numerous women at once, romancing them and promising marriage when he retired. He thought he had life made as a "player." Unfortunately, he got cut from the team when one computer-savvy lady became suspicious and hacked into his hotmail account. She found all the other women and group-emailed them the truth. Fakers get caught eventually.

The choice for those of you who might want to fake sincerity in your relationships is fairly straightforward. You could be honest, separate at age 30 or 40 and have a chance of finding someone more suitable for you at a relatively youthful age; or you could stay in denial and delay the eventual reckoning until you're 50 or 60 — at which time you will have lost a decade or two out of your short little life. Use this book to help you find out what you want, not to cheat your wife and yourself out of precious years.

The most important thing is deciding what you really want. Is she the woman for you? Do her attitudes and goals mesh with yours? Would you prefer someone who is more youthful and energetic? Someone easier to get along with? There's no use fighting to keep a marriage alive if you're not really invested in it for the long-term. "To thine own self, be true" means just that, so tell yourself the truth. Use this time to help reveal it, not to hide from it.

Be creative: think outside the box

Even if you read the *Mars and Venus* series until you've memorized its contents word for word, there's no guarantee that listening actively, communicating your feelings, or other Mars/Venus techniques will rejuvenate a failing marriage. Once the veneer of caring has cracked, it takes more than a quick coat of varnish to change her perceptions about you. With luck, it's not too late.

The sad fact is that everybody puts other people into boxes and labels them. This is not malicious. It's just one way in which people save time in their social interactions. At work, people box us in very quickly. In marriages, over time we develop assumptions and opinions about our partners, in-laws and kids that color our thinking toward them, i.e., we box them in. Your wife has already done this. You have done this.

Your job is to think outside the box — more specifically, to develop creative ways to change your wife's perception of you. And in the meantime you must start thinking about how to change your perception of her.

This is hard to do — for all of us. Once a perception is set (he doesn't like spending time with the kids; she doesn't really love me; he's always late; she doesn't like sex; he would rather watch basketball than talk to me) it can be hard to change. It takes a long and continuous period of altered behavior before change can be trusted.

> POINT
> Don't quit too early — give this process a fair chance

Many men no doubt have made sincere efforts to address the perception problem and make adjustments. But failure often results when they have high expectations of a quick payback. If their wife doesn't respond right away they may quit far too early in the process. Give it a chance. It could take months or even a year or two.

Right or wrong, your wife's poor perception of you has developed as a result of many negative incidents over time. It will take many more positive incidents to get you back to square one, and then additional positive actions to build up credits in her bank. This all takes patience and, depending on the state of your relationship, perhaps a great deal of time.

Stand up like a man

Okay, so you want your marriage to succeed but maybe you're already giving in a lot. Perhaps the strategies you're employing are the wrong ones. Maybe your marriage theme has been to play the wussy. Are you doing a lot of kissing up and plenty of "yes, dear; yes, dear" in an effort to keep the relationship going? Are you giving way too much in the marriage? (If so, there are quite a few women I know who'd like to meet you!) Really, this has got to stop. Your wife could be losing her attraction to you.

We all know people who don't stand up for themselves or who are too "nice"; it's a sad fact of life that they don't get as much respect as they deserve. You don't want to be known simply as a nice guy. You need to take a good, hard look at how you interact with your wife and project yourself in front of her. Then consider if, in addition to being the guy who opens the door for her, you're also the doormat.

If that's the case, you need to decide where fair is and draw the line. Don't accept treatment that isn't fair and don't do things that aren't fair. Stand up for what you believe. Women respect a man who stands up for himself. If you give away your personal power, disrespect is only a heartbeat away.

However, standing up for yourself is a critical strategy that should be implemented with care. If you choose to move forward with this, do so slowly and gradually. Be sure to stand up for yourself in everything, not just your marriage. The actor Kevin Spacey plays the lead role in the movie *American Beauty*, in which the husband suddenly realizes he has been a wimp at work and at home, and starts standing up for himself. It's entertaining, but he seems to push for too much change too quickly. Not to give it away, but there are severe repercussions for him in doing this. The lesson in standing up for yourself is to proceed with caution. If you're too much of a nice guy, check out the book *No More Mr. Nice Guy* to get a handle on the problem.

Get a relationship counselor you both respect

If the marriage is having serious problems and you are unable to communicate without falling into well-worn patterns of conflict, you should get someone to act as a mediator to reframe how you talk and — even more importantly — listen to each other. The good ones can help you reset how you communicate. There are professional marriage mediators in the yellow pages, or your family doctor may have contacts in this area. You can also check with the American Association for Marriage and Family Therapy (www.aamft.org) for an accredited counselor near you. Friends are another source. The thing to remember is that the person must connect with both of you. If one of you doesn't feel comfortable with the counselor, you need to keep looking.

I was fortunate in that a friend recommended a relationship counselor who was perfect for both of us and continues to be a family friend to this day. There are many quality relationship counselors who can help you mend your marriage or ease your separation.

Faith and relationships: the devout wife

I once met a couple at a resort who were attending a marriage weekend seminar through their church. The husband (it was his second marriage) was ecstatic, as anyone would be after attending such an inspirational event. His wife, however, took the opportunity to casually mention that she felt lonely in the relationship. This sign of disconnect was a bad omen.

What I took from this is that men can't assume, simply because they attend sessions on marriage-building through church, the community or a family counselor, that the relationship will automatically be strengthened.

The reason is that, while following church teachings on marriage can be of real help in creating a long-lasting relationship, building a sound marriage must include addressing a woman's needs for equality, intimacy and connection with *you*.

It is critical that men ensure their skills in the relationship be centered as much on their partner's needs for intimate connection as they are faith-focused.

Consider a question. Have you used faith-based or other marriage support counseling but skirted another important issue: the need to enhance your skills, personal want-to and abilities in building intimacy and emotional connection in the relationship? There is no shortcut. You must build a tangible connection with your wife or she will continue to feel "alone" in the relationship.

B. DAY-TO-DAY PLAYS

Okay, now let's get down to the nitty-gritty: the little, day-to-day things that can make or break a relationship. These may sound insignificant, but you know they're not.

Right now, stop doing three things that really annoy her

The 80/20 principle applied to a marriage means that 80 per cent of the irritation could be caused by just a few trouble spots (the 20 per cent). Here's how it works: if your wife had a top-ten list of things you do that she really dislikes, odds are the top two (20 per cent) on her list would account for 80 per cent of her hard feelings.

So, right off the bat, think of the various things you do that might annoy her — hopefully there aren't too many — and try to stop doing three of them. This could greatly reduce the trouble in your marriage, far out of proportion to the work you might put in to correct them. Begin with the most irritating.

What should you stop doing? It depends. What bugs her the most? Perhaps you always leave the toilet seat lid up, spend money or drink like a drunken sailor, forget to put away the peanut butter jar when you're finished with it, are continually late, or don't shower often enough. As in most things in life, the bulk of these behaviors can be corrected by simple free will. It could be that you choose not to spend enough time with your kids, avoid looking her in the eye when she talks to you, or regularly forget to take out the garbage. The point is, identify three significant annoyances and make the choice to stop or start doing whatever will fix the problem.

Glasser's seven deadly sins (criticizing, blaming, complaining, nagging, threatening, punishing, and bribing or rewarding to control) may be a good place to start. Are any of these part of your regular relationship routine?

If you feel ambitious and can think of ten things to change, even better — but begin with the ones that will have the greatest impact on her in the short-term. There's no time to lose, you've got a relationship to rebuild.

Clean up your financial troubles

This is a biggie. Overspending is a huge source of marital irritation. As Joe Garagiola once said, "I know a baseball player who wouldn't report the theft of his wife's credit cards because the thief spends less than she does." Hey, maybe *you're* the family spendthrift.

More than overspending, financial security and saving are critical for most women, especially beginning in their late 30s when thoughts of funding retirement come to the fore. The reason is, women can live up to ten years longer than men, and so they need to save a lot more to carry them through those extra years. The retirement clock ticks louder and longer for women.

My friend Jim just couldn't help spending. He and his wife were constantly in debt to the credit card companies. Nothing outrageous, but they couldn't get ahead. She was a saver who was never able to put anything away. It was a wedge issue that eventually played a key part in the separation: when she was losing her attachment to him, the financial aspect tipped the balance more heavily toward leaving.

Take Mark, who preferred to have the high-flying, exciting-but-unstable sales jobs that demanded long hours, rather than the more stable employment and financial certainty his wife needed. Much of their trouble stemmed from her feelings of stress. Changing to a more stable but less glamorous job might be just the fix your relationship needs. Every guy has to ask himself this: what does she really need and how much do I want to help her get it?

As for me, my ex and I are both savers so financials were not a traumatic concern. However, now that we're separated money is much tighter, as we're paying for two households — but it could have been even worse. The financial repercussions are another reason (if you really need one) to work very hard to make your relationship succeed.

Either partner can be guilty of excessive spending. If it's you, it's imperative you rein in your spending and start paying off your debts, starting with the high-interest-rate credit card bills first. Your wife will notice this quickly and you will have reduced a major source of marital angst — see the 80/20 rule above. This could be one of the most valuable changes you make.

Be on time

This is a gargantuan issue for many women. Husbands who say they'll be home at five o'clock and drop in at 6:15 after having stopped off for a quick beer. Or who don't call when they're going to be late, even by just a few minutes. This becomes especially problematic when she can set her clock by your being late. It's akin to coming straight out and telling someone that you don't view their time as important, that it's okay to make them wait.

One friend, Leslie, told me she used to worry a lot in the early years of her marriage when her husband didn't come home from basketball for hours after she knew the games were over. He would finally show up in the early morning hours. She knew he was probably okay but she didn't stop worrying — until she began to view it as disrespectful. She promptly ceased fretting, turned off the lights and went to bed; it was a key factor in their eventual separation. Always being a few minutes late may have played a role in my breakup (doh!); don't let it play a role in yours.

Surprise your partner: make the choice to be on time from this point forward. For *everything*. If you're going to be late, call. The fact that you've done so shows her you're not taking her for granted. And don't just dabble in improving in this area — actually change! If you settle for being five minutes late all the time, she'll put you back in that box — and you'll have no one to blame but yourself.

On the other hand, be a bit unpredictable and mysterious
No, this doesn't mean keeping her guessing by showing up late! There's no doubt that one of the essential elements in a successful marriage with kids is a certain element of predictability and routine. That's why she selected you as a mate. However, the same things that are vital to the marriage (routine, predictability, comfort) naturally get a little stale after a few years. We all need the spontaneity and excitement that comes from doing unusual things at odd times.

You need to strike a balance between "routineness" and "spontaneity." Keep the predictability needed for the partnership to function (be on time, take care of your chores, etc.), but start adding some excitement to the relationship. Bring flowers home unexpectedly, invite her along on a business trip, or suggest a romantic interlude. You get the picture. She may not want to do any of these things, but provided you're not pushy your efforts will help to keep her from contracting the often fatal "predictable husband/bored wife syndrome." As in most things in life, there is value in the effort.

Get some manners

"Please" and "thank you" go a long way. Pay attention to your wife when she talks to you. Put the toilet seat down. Flush the toilet. Make the bed. Put your clothes away. Say "excuse me" after burping or, better yet, don't burp in front of her. You know what's needed here. If you act like a swine, all you'll be good for is bringing home the bacon. But if she makes more money than you — ah well, that's when you can get dropped from the team.

Curb your snoring and other bodily functions

If you snore, get help. Sometimes this is caused by a simple, recurring sinus infection that can be cured in a week or two with medication. Then again, it may require an operation. Sometimes just losing twenty or thirty pounds will do the trick. Again, making the effort scores points. Same thing with passing gas, burping and other bodily functions. This stuff is funny with eight-year-old boys, but that's just about where its value ends. On the other hand, if she can recite the alphabet in one long burp...

Don't sweat the small stuff

Does it really matter if the toilet paper rolls out from the bottom or from than the top? I no longer let this type of valueless debate get in the way of my happiness because, as important as saving TP may be, it's not worth fighting over. (I say it shouldn't be a problem anyway, as *everyone* knows you save two squares of tissue per usage if you roll it out from the top! But I digress.) Don't sweat the small things that crop up every day. Instead, work on the big items.

Avoid the "married singles" trap

Are you becoming "married singles" — still a couple but each doing their own thing, living almost separate lives under the same roof? Don't make the common error of celebrating this as "independence" or "freedom." You may end up with more freedom than you'd like.

The answer is to develop some shared interests — and fast. Decorating, gardening, gourmet cooking, walking, golf, running — believe it or not, women have strong interests in many things besides their husbands and children. Want to keep your marriage thriving? Find one or two things that she loves and get involved. Having a joint hobby or activity is one of the very best ways to stay connected.

"What about our children?" you may be asking. It's true that for many years children can be a couple's principal shared hobby. Still, as kids grow older and further away from you, even this "hobby" can slide away. It's imperative you find other activities to share with your wife because, once the kids are gone, you're left staring at each other.

C. GIFTING/ROMANCE

When she says she doesn't like gifts, flowers or chocolate, don't believe her. Everyone appreciates gifts and romance. Use the tips below to optimize your efforts.

If your best buddy called and said he had two tickets to tonight's football game, you'd be pretty happy about getting the surprise gift. No doubt your wife would feel the same (except maybe for the part about football). Romance involves many little surprises that show a man cares. In fact, for women the surprise (not the gift) is the big attraction, as it lets her know you've been thinking about her. Catching her off guard is one of your best plays, so don't be a dummy and advertise the fact that you're about to do something fun and romantic: you'll only succeed in killing the impact.

Also, what's the use of giving your woman a gift she doesn't love? Find out what she really likes and give her something memorable. It doesn't have to be expensive either. If the present is unique and thoughtful about her, it's like making the game-winning TD catch one-handed with the cornerback draped all over you. If it's handmade and also says something about your relationship — well, look out! Surprise is the key here to warming her heart. Couldn't we all use a heartwarming gift now and then?

One exception to this rule is when you're buying something significant, like a ring. Don't buy an expensive item unless you are absolutely certain — confirmed by her close friend or even her if possible — that it's something she will love.

A creative way to deal with an expensive item is give her a card saying that you will be taking her out to buy it. Give her a heads-up and let her get involved in getting the item she really wants — rather than the wrong one you will almost certainly select if you buy it by yourself.

Note: Don't make the mistake of giving gifts in lieu of active communication or your time and attention, as this will infuriate her. No woman wants to feel she is being bought off, and most will recognize shallow attempts to curry favor.

Birthdays, Christmas, Mother's Day

The key is to always give gifts that are romantic and personal, items that demonstrate you put a little effort and feeling into it. Avoid giving "useful" gifts such as kitchen appliances or power tools, no matter how badly these are needed around the house. If she requests these, consider this is a "trap" designed to confirm to her that you have no concept of romance; if you fall for this, you deserve your fate. But, then again, maybe she likes practical gifts. Pay attention to your wife to know for sure.

Until you have spent some time developing a sense of what types of gifts she will value (by listening carefully to her subtle hints and keeping track of them), it's hard to go wrong with a gift certificate for a spa treatment, massage or manicure, if she's into that kind of thing. Or perhaps give her a card that focuses on something unique about her. Greeting cards and thoughtful notes are always good, especially if you add a personal touch. There are plenty of gift ideas that will convey meaning to her. For mothers, one of the best choices is a weekend getaway at a nice hotel, with all the details of child- and/or pet-sitting prearranged by you.

Valentine's Day is romantic quicksand

"Oops, tomorrow is Valentine's Day!" Better run out and grab a card and a box of chocolates/dozen roses/dinner invitation and show your wife how much you "love" her, right? Once a year: the foundation of a successful relationship. Wrong. Man, oh man, I'm guilty as charged on this one. Hey, no excuses, but it seemed okay because that's what my dad did.

Buddy, you're scoring major demerit points for doing the same old tired gift-giving on a "Hallmark holiday." Just because the tradition (promoted by the card, flower and chocolate companies) is that you give a card and candy on February 14, it doesn't mean you have to be Pavlov's dog and drool on command. I give you permission to break the rules. Your wife might love something different.

But what? This is the question that really haunts men. It can actually appear to make better sense to get the same-old, same-old gift, which the wife at least expects, rather than try something new and be confirmed as a guy who really doesn't know his partner at all. But appearances, as always, can be deceiving.

The key to success at birthdays, Christmas and Valentine's Day is to refer to your notes taken over the course of the year to develop a good list of creative gift ideas. One way to find out what she might like is to offer to go shopping with her now and then. Plus, she will love the fact that you want to go with her — think of this not as shopping but as marriage insurance.

Remember, the best gifts demonstrate to her that you've been paying attention. Since Valentine's Day is a romance occasion, your gift must say something special about your relationship. This could range from things she has pointed out over the course of the year to favorite CDs. Over time, you'll get a sense of the things she'd like. Typically, they might include candles, candleholders, well-chosen books, bath products, lingerie, picture frames (maybe with your kids' photos included), a promise to redecorate the living room — the list goes on.

Clothing can be a risky area unless you are really in tune with your wife's tastes and her size. Also, if your wife is environmentally conscious, she'll prefer "consumables," things that can be used up and their packaging recycled, such as the bath products and candles mentioned above.

Here's a radical idea to get you brainstorming about your own unique gift. In the second week of January, give her a unique card with a note inside that reads, "I couldn't wait until Valentines Day!" Then, give her a small gift each week from the list of things she's shown interest in over the year. Culminate this effort in a surprise weekend away at her favorite resort the week before Valentine's Day.

On the big day, do something very understated, like taking the kids away for a couple of hours or making breakfast in the morning. Find a chore she doesn't like to do and do it for her. (Of course, this chore idea can be implemented all year.) Add in a small, thoughtful note, then leave her to enjoy your efforts. Odds are she'll be bragging about you to her friends.

By now you should be getting the picture. Be creative; think outside the box. Do the unexpected. Show you care. Keep her off guard, wondering, anticipating what you might do next. Work at it. The last point is key. Show her you're making some effort and you're halfway there. The magical thing is that, as you do this, you gradually build up your skills (think golf swing) and romantic actions come more easily. Slowly but surely you can become naturally romantic just as you now "naturally" roll those long putts in. Don't hold back — it's actually quite enjoyable, and not that hard to do.

One more thing, if you do buy chocolates on Valentine's Day, really think about what she likes. If she can't stand fancy centers, it would be pointless to buy these. If she loves chocolate but is dieting, buy something very small but of excellent quality, to show her you care about her goals but think she deserves a bit of luxury once in a while.

Further reading: Not great at brainstorming fun, romantic things to do for your wife? Check out *1001 Ways to Be Romantic* by Gregory Godek and *The RoMANtic's Guide* by Michael Webb. These books have loads of great, and often low-cost, ideas for injecting romance into your life. Keep in mind, though, that romance is not just about the things you do — it's about developing a feeling for what your partner would love. Romance will often fall spontaneously out of that focused attention.

Final point: consider how you can make every day Valentine's Day through small, thoughtful gifts like helping out around the house.

Go back to your good old days

No, not the John Wayne Era. Think back to when you were dating. You looked for, hunted for, trinkets, little events, shared moments, anything that would draw you closer to her. These became tiny connection points that helped her feel close — and helped *you* get close! Of course, it was partially hormone-driven, but there was probably also a powerful thinking/emotional human connection that was spiritual in nature. You were attracted to her physically, but you also had the lure of a deeper, lasting connection.

Over time in a marriage, the connection points change. Kids come along, diapers get changed, and you don't go for long walks together holding hands as much. You grow apart from those heady early days when you literally couldn't get close enough. Yet most of us long for the close contact of those days and often the memory of them keeps a marriage together long after it's over. Sadly, wives and husbands get into affairs looking to rekindle the excitement and connection of the early days.

Think back to a time (lasting longer than a couple of months) when you were really happy in your relationship. Possibly this was before you had children. Now remember some of the things you did together that built a connection with your wife. It could be running your fingers through her hair when you first kissed her or told her what great eyes she had. It may be the first time you danced with her, or the walks you took together. These will always have a special, symbolic meaning for both of you. Think about how you can start doing some of these things again. Refer back to the exercise starting on page 54.

Real men give flowers

Women love flowers, especially cut flowers that are expensive and die within a few days! But buying flowers is a symbol of love — always has been — and that's why real men give flowers. Looking for flowers that match her choice of decorating colors is a good start. Also, the next time she puts flowers in a vase, check out the various colors and types of flowers she has chosen for herself. Write this down in your notes section so that you can buy similar (but not identical) ones in the future.

I don't advocate buying flowers for her birthday or Mother's Day — she'll view this as a duty call — but the other fifty weeks of the year are fair game. If you haven't bought flowers for a while, she'll think you've been a bad boy and are feeling guilty. Also, don't give her flowers within a few days of her having done something for you. She'll think you're rewarding her and the impact will be lessened. The only reason for giving a woman flowers is "because I was thinking about you today" or a similar reason expressed with sincerity.

"Plan" to be spontaneous

Train yourself to plan for "last-minute" getaways and "spontaneous" dinners — anything thoughtful to break up the daily grind. Take a lesson from the example shown in this TV commercial: a woman is driving her husband to the airport for yet another business trip. She is in a sour mood, perhaps because he is going to Paris without her. When they arrive at the airport and she opens the trunk of the car, she discovers two suitcases, his and hers. She is going to France with him! He has combined a surprise with a last-minute getaway that says "I've been thinking about you." Magic.

One of the biggest complaints women have is about husbands who sit around the house all day, watching sports or reading the paper. Boring. Once you become predictable to your wife, you get put into that box, labeled and maybe even buried.

One friend has a habit of spending days in advance making elaborate "last-minute" plans to go away to a nearby mountain resort with his wife. He moves his afternoon appointments to another day, phones ahead to make sure he can get the hotel suite he wants, ensures that his wife has nothing pressing on, and lines up a babysitter. Then he casually phones her mid-morning to say, "Hey, let's go away overnight — tonight." When she raises the usual objections — no babysitter, his work, etc., he easily counters each one. They leave within a couple of hours. In football terminology, he's now in the red zone!

Last-minute suggestions for fun can be very attractive to your wife. Approaching sex a different way (taking longer than five minutes, kissing her softly instead of like a bear, taking your time in foreplay) is another idea. Be ready with an answer when her curiosity gets the better of her and she asks, "Why are you acting differently — did you do something wrong?" She may wonder if you're having an affair.

For the sake of your relationship, build in a little spontaneity. It doesn't have to be a trip to Paris or a mountain resort. It could be going out for dinner, a weekend away at a friend's cottage, or just a last-second trip to see a movie or get ice cream. Be creative. Start planning to be spontaneous.

Accept that women won't tell you how to romance them

Many women believe that discovery and detective work is part of romance; they want to see some initiative from you. Your doing a little investigative work to discover more about them is a big part of the magic and mystery of romance. To draw you a complete road map would leave her feeling uncertain about the sincerity of your actions. I think most women would agree that this could compromise trust.

Don't get disheartened if all this appears to be too much work. It's not that much once you develop your skills. The key to her heart is hidden in plain view! That said, she's not going to give it away; you've got to work a bit for it.

But remember that you're not flying blind. They know you need help so they drop little clues here and there. They want you to succeed. Once you get your "paying attention" skills up to speed, you're in a good position to catch the clues and enjoy the fun in romance.

The forbidden "R" word

In romance, when all is said and done, a lot more is said than done.

When deciding to become more romantic, the most important point is less talk, more action. Once at a dinner party, the host asked everyone to identify a goal for the coming year. When it was his turn, he told everyone he planned to "be more romantic."

Now, that's an excellent goal. In fact, it's what this book is all about. Yet, the public statement in front of his wife may have been a mistake. The heads-up to her meant that now she might be on the lookout for him "being romantic." If she is harboring any ill will toward his romance skills, she will be ready to grade the effort immediately. He has just raised the bar for himself.

The best romance is comprised of subtle yet self-assured acts. Let your actions say it for you.

D. THE PHYSICAL SIDE

These tips are about a whole lot more than just sex, so be sure to read carefully.

Get physical with your wife

If you're trying to rejuvenate a marriage, one of the foundations is to get more physical. Again, this isn't about the horizontal dance, wrestling or touch football. It's about trying to find an avenue for engaging in physical fitness together in order to foster a lasting bond. It could be cycling, golf, rock climbing, canoeing, dancing, walking or bowling; the possibilities are endless. What does she like to do? Find something that can work for both of you. The point is that she wants your focused attention, and exercising together is a perfect way to remove domestic distractions and improve your physical fitness level. And, if you're a little or a lot overweight, exercise will help melt away those extra pounds.

Do more non-sexual touching

Touching her shoulder, holding hands, hugging, foot rubs, playing with her hair — they're all small but vital steps to rekindling your relationship. However, prior to trying any of these you must carefully gauge your wife's attachment to you. Attempting to hold hands or hug her when she's furious with you will only hurt your cause.

That said, if you're not doing much non-sexual touching then it's an area to target for improvement. Going with your wife for regular walks creates the perfect opportunity for "accidentally" touching her or casually holding hands.

Learn to dance (properly)

For those many men who never learned to dance or who feel self-conscious on the dance floor, you're missing a great opportunity to develop a skill you can share with your wife for decades.

It starts at a young age. Allison, a young waitress, lives with her boyfriend and has studied dance all her life. Dancing is a part of who she is. He's a firefighter who refuses to get up on the dance floor, even for some close dancing. They're on track to get married and have kids, and he's missing a great chance to build a stronger bond with her by getting involved in something she loves. It may not fit the firefighter tough-guy image he fosters for himself, but if he put the same amount of energy into learning how to dance as he does into his work, she would be one very happy camper.

The lesson here: take some dance lessons with your partner. Putting aside the fact that you might become a good dancer and get more physically fit, a night of close dancing could be just what's needed to re-energize your relationship.

It's hug time

If your father wasn't a hugger, you may not be either. But physical contact is essential for staying connected to your wife and kids. With your wife, start with hand-holding before working your way to hugs. Another way to get started is to simply ask for a hug, or say to her, "I could sure use a hug right now" or "You look like you could use a hug." This works well with my kids. My daughter once said, in response to my saying I thought she could use a hug, "How did you know? I needed a hug so badly I was ready to hug my teacher!" If you're uncomfortable hugging your wife in broad daylight, wait until night and the lights are low before moving on to this. Do this in a place where she won't interpret your effort as a play for sex. Of course, you'll want to start hugging your kids right away — if they'll let you.

Kissing: the light touch

If your wife wanted a big sloppy, in-your-face kiss, she'd whistle for the family dog. Most women are highly attuned to touch. Their skin is very sensitive. What you consider a light kiss can come across to her as brutish. Plus, even your best shave could leave a five o'clock shadow that can give her a bad case of whisker burn that...well, burns. Forget all those movies you've seen. While women will once in a while want a teeth-chipping kiss, most of the time they don't.

When you next kiss her, experiment by kissing more lightly and slowly than usual. Also, build her anticipation by not kissing her right away. Delay slightly. You almost want to tease her, but not so much that she catches on to what you're doing. Anticipation of a kiss is almost as important as the kiss itself.

Most quality "how to make love to a woman" books spend a lot of time on the importance of kissing. Read one or two of these books and put them into practice. One you should check out is *How to Give Her Absolute Pleasure* by Lou Paget. This book is worthwhile reading and is one of a series by the author.

Finally, never, ever give or allow her to give you a "sister" kiss (the kind of peck you give your sibling when you see her). Kissing should always convey passion and sexual interest. If it's going to be a sister kiss in the morning, add something else, like looking into her eyes meaningfully or rubbing her forearm. Keep your relationship special. Oh, and if you want her to enjoy your kissing more, surprise her with the gift of shaving very closely just before you get together. Even if you have a very heavy beard growth and go through razors often, her appreciation will be worth it.

Sex: ladies first

Here's an old guys' joke. Question: How do I know when my wife has had an orgasm? Answer: I don't, I'm usually making pancakes by then.

A bit insensitive, but probably true of the "good old days" and perhaps even today, especially for those who are little bored or lazy in their relationships. It was likely true of our fathers before the 1960s, when women's sexual needs first gained public attention — well, except for the part about the man making breakfast: the woman was expected to do that too.

Today, however, the days of men first — or worse, men only — should be over. In today's game, you must take good care of your woman. To do that, you need to slow down. Take your time undressing her. What's the rush? Now, slowing down doesn't necessarily mean you have to become an expert in tantric techniques, or have intercourse for two hours instead of your customary two minutes! However, experts like Paget say it means lots of time spent enjoying foreplay.

Foreplay starts during everyday life. When you see her looking good, don't just look out the window when you're talking to her. Look her in the eye, then glance at her body so she'll know you've noticed. Tell her what you like about her. In your single days, you probably did this without thinking. Now that you're an established couple, you've probably slipped up; you need to continue conveying your interest.

Don't overdo this, just let her know that you're interested in her physically and sexually. Keep doing these and other little romantic touches to keep the heart fires burning. Gauge what she likes. Don't come on like a lecher (unless she enjoys that!).

Speaking of what she likes, feel free to ask her what she wants in sex. Or simply pay better attention and note the not-so-subtle hints she drops as you go along.

For most women, sex (beginning with kissing) should move slowly. Women consider the light, sensuous touching and kissing of foreplay to be a core part of the experience; it's the bridge between their romantic attachment to a man and their connection to him physically. The man who understands this and delivers on it will find his wife developing a deeper desire for him. Allow her to become excited with anticipation well before you touch her. That'll get you going too.

However, let's face it, taking your time goes against the caveman/movie-cowboy grain. The dichotomy is that men are quick, while women want it done "sloooowly." It's the man's obligation to take his time in the process of sex — my suggestion is to take two to four times longer in each area than you do currently. Then see how she reacts to find out whether you need to go slower still, or speed up a bit. If she's falling asleep, then you might want to pick up the pace.

The subject of sex could make a whole series of books. As mentioned, there are a number of excellent how-to guides by experts on this topic, so check out the relationship section of your local bookstore. Purchase them online if you don't want to buy them in public. Read all you want, but remember that the sexiest thing to a woman is that you're interested, paying attention, responding to her signals about what she likes, and taking your time.

Here's one final point: when (if) she shows she likes your enhanced kissing skills, suggest you go to the bookstore together to buy a book or two on this topic. Expanding your sexual repertoire together could turn out to be a great shared hobby.

E. COMMUNICATING

One of the top complaints women have against us, right? Well, they're spot on. Don't let your male ego rob your relationship of true communication. Key: always think of talking not as information exchange, but as a way to build connection with her.

Say "I love you"

Some people find this tough. Many men have trouble saying these words to their loved ones. Yet, in a committed relationship, they are golden. Many of the tips and actions listed in this section demonstrate that you love her. Now you need to say it, sincerely. For those of us who have trouble saying these words — maybe because our fathers didn't show us how by telling our mothers in front of us — here's how you can get better and feel more at ease with this magic phrase.

Since it's always easier to talk about tough matters in the dark, go to bed early so that you're not sound asleep by the time you hit the pillow. You can sneak in your early I-love-yous to her when you're in bed and both about to go to sleep. The next time you're in bed with her, just say, "Ok, have a great sleep, I love you."

Another one is when you're sending her off somewhere and she's just about to leave. You can slip in the I-love-you at the start of a comment (so that it doesn't just hang there at the end leaving you feeling goofy). For example, "You're off? Okay, love you, have a great time, say hi to everyone for me. Tell your dad I want a rematch!"

No matter how you say it, she will probably notice. She may respond with questions. Or perhaps she will do a double-take. If the former, be ready with a good answer. If she says something like, "Why did you say 'I love you'?" keep the answer short. "Because it's true." Less is more.

Don't make a big deal out of it; it's just a phrase (but obviously more than that and something we all should say to our loved ones even if it's tough to get started). Once you begin you'll never look back. And you'll be teaching your kids how to use these words in the future. It's something worth doing for that reason alone.

Speaking of your kids, when was the last time you told them you loved them? Best to start when they're little and never stop, as it can be a little uncomfortable trying to start this when they are older and beginning to distance themselves from you. Same thing with hugs, by the way. When I put my son and daughter to bed at night, I say "I love you" with a hug as the last thing. I know they're learning — and remembering. I'll never stop doing this, because it's important and also because I know it might be too hard to start up again if I stop.

Tell her you were thinking of her

Women love it when they know you were thinking of her while at work or play. Of course, you think about her a fair bit (at halftime, right? — just kidding!). Take the time to let her know it. It's a small action with big impact. This is best done through a quick phone call or email.

Brag about her

Is she great with the kids, does she keep herself in great shape, is she an excellent cook, is she smart, funny or just plain fun? Take time out often to brag about her to people. Do it in front of her as long as it's not grandstanding. It shows that you care and appreciate what she's all about.

Say thank you

She's carried and delivered your children, and is raising and nuturing them along with looking after a thousand household duties. Maybe she's helped you through personal battles. A sincere thank you, with cut flowers and a romantic dinner — just to show appreciation — will convey to her how much you care. When in doubt, say thank you or show it.

Say "I feel," not "I think"

Men have been trained to be rational "thinking" beings. We often don't talk or even think about feelings — and even when we do we frequently fail to recognize it. Women are very receptive to feeling-and-emotion conversations. Often, miscommunication occurs simply because the man is using rational language even when he's talking about feelings. Since he lives in a man's world, he's learned to couch his feelings in rational language. Unless she is highly intuitive, the woman may miss this.

Here's a suggestion. In conversations with your wife, stop using the sentence starter "I think" and replace it with "I feel" or "I sense." Always lead with "I feel," as in "I feel we need to spend more time together," or "I sense the Red Sox and Cubs will meet in the World Series this year."

Now, if using "I feel" is too big a leap for you, a halfway point is to use "my sense is" as a softener, e.g., "My sense is that I need to spend more time with the kids." Give it a try. It delivers a warmer, softer tone to your relationship style that your partner will notice and appreciate. Try it and see if you get results.

On another note, in business meetings or other alpha settings, using "I sense" or "my sense is" is a good way to bring up "I think" or "feeling" points without coming across as too strident or touchy-feely. It's a smooth form of communicating that can build bridges to others.

EXERCISE

Observe yourself at home and work and see how often you say "I think" when you're really giving your feeling, intuition or best guess on something. Try to get an idea of how "I feel" or "I sense" would fit in those spots. Start using those words more and see if there's a difference. When

> QUESTION
> What's the difference between women's intuition and men's "gut instinct"? Answer: Nothing, they're exactly the same except that no woman will ever admit she has a gut! Hence, the word intuition was invented. Men are capable of intuition if they work at it.

you're trying to figure something out in your home life or at work, ask yourself, "What's my sense of how this will go?"; it just takes some getting used to.

Listen!

This point cannot be overstressed. As mentioned, communication involves listening as much as talking. The biggest myth in our talkshow-based, me-oriented society is that communication is about talking and expressing yourself, being heard above the noise of everyone else. In fact, communication is about two-way interaction. If you want to learn more about what sets your wife's soul on fire, let her do the talking. Listen actively. And don't forget to take notes if you've got a foggy memory!

Here's a technique for listening actively and getting her to keep talking. Listen to what she says and identify her key points. Try to connect it to the feeling she having. Here's an example.

She: "My dad called and he seemed really unhappy. I can't stop thinking about it."

He: "What was it that upset you?"

She: "It made me think about how Mom used to be there for him…."

He: "Yeah, that's got to be hard for him. Do you think he feels like he doesn't have much support?"

By connecting your wife's comment to the emotion she is experiencing, you are validating her feelings — something she will appreciate. It will also give you a bit of time to think clearly about what she is saying, and say something meaningful back to her. Listening — active listening during which you're focused on understanding what she has to say rather than on thinking about what you will say next or how to end the conversation quickly — is the foundation of effective two-way communication.

She will also appreciate your not attempting to explain away her concerns or solve her problems for her (e.g., "Oh, you shouldn't worry about him. He has your sister and his two neighbors fussing over him, doesn't he? But if it makes you feel better, let's invite him to come and stay for a week. You'll both feel better and then you can stop letting this get to you. There, problem solved."). Remember, she just wants to express herself, and will not appreciate your seemingly simple fix. General law of relationships: never try to solve her problems unless she specifically requests your help.

Learn to self-disclose

This is another toughie for men. Self-disclosure means just that. Women are better at self-disclosure than men and often find the give and take out of balance: they've "disclosed," while their man is just plain "closed."

An imbalance in disclosure leads eventually to a relationship gap. The key to rebuilding your relationship is to even out that imbalance. If you want to keep your relationship energized, you have to start talking personally about yourself: your fears, your hopes and your dreams. Easier said than done, but start with small stuff or work talk and gradually build up to more personal matters. You won't believe how she will respond to this — as long as you stay with it over a period of time. Sincerity is vital.

EXERCISE

Begin a sentence with the word "I" and then tell her something important or scary about you. It doesn't have to be your life's greatest fear. Start small and work up to more important matters as your comfort level increases. You can also do this with your kids to build a great connection.

Connecting versus bonding

Further to self-disclosing, we men often mistakenly believe that by talking about how sad/angry we were about our team losing the game, or discussing the house or the car, we are "connecting" with our wives. In reality, this is only attempted male bonding with a female. The truth is, for women to build a lasting emotional link with you, you must talk about personal matters, feelings and experiences. If you know that self-disclosing is needed to make your marriage team win, make it worthwhile and go beyond bonding. You know what to do. Make like an athlete and *Just Do It!*

Be strategically honest

As valuable as being totally honest with her may be, there are times in your relationship when this will do more harm than good. This is when you need to use "strategic" honesty. That is, you don't have to tell her everything when she asks. As good a relationship as you think you have with her — where you "talk about everything and have no secrets" — you would be advised to avoid letting her know how hard you're working on the relationship and your romance skills. A little mystery adds spice.

If she knows you're doing something different to make the relationship better, she will naturally be curious and looking for whatever it is you're doing differently. She might then begin to discount your efforts. When that occurs, she will look at it rationally (he's trying to be romantic) instead of absorbing it through her senses (and saying to herself, "I'm feeling good about him"). This can harm your entire effort.

> **WARNING**
> Once you start, there's no going back

In order to improve your relationship (because you have to do some things she mustn't know you're doing), you need to keep a low profile and tailor your actions to impress her. The goal here is pure — building a marriage that will be successful — but the means may appear manipulative. Look at this as a "white lie" for the greater good — as long as you're sincere in your ultimate objectives.

F. CAUTIONARY TIPS

Before you start implementing the techniques you think will improve your relationship, take a minute to make note of the following common-sense warnings. How you implement your changes can be just as important as what changes you select.

Okay, let's cut to the chase. Men know instinctively that if we start doing things with our wife or for her, it becomes very hard to go back on this precedent. Many avoid doing things that might set a standard. However, nobody ever said having a good marriage was going to be easy, so it's probably time you got over this one.

Given the possibly fragile state of your relationship, it is critical any positive change you make be continued. You are better off just doing one thing really well and consistently rather than trying to do too much and not succeeding at anything. Your wife will focus on your backsliding right away and any headway you've made will be lost.

Don't rush your changes

On the other hand, change too quickly and she may get suspicious. She may wonder if you're having an affair (false). Worse still, she may think you're deliberately changing things up to impress her (true). The reality is that you're also making these changes for yourself. Try to get a sense of how fast to proceed with change. It won't take much to start creating an impression, so don't feel you have to rush.

And don't be too obvious!

One of the dangers of deciding to work on your relationship is that you suddenly become converted on the road to Damascus, turn over a new leaf and begin trying to make it up to your wife very quickly. As she is likely totally tuned in to your well-worn act, any big change from your previous behavior and persona may be met with skepticism and mistrust. Seriously, you'll have some explaining to do, and no matter what you say she'll be watching you carefully from then on.

A friend tells me that one time, just to shake things up, he did the laundry and made the bed for his wife. She almost had heart failure and thought he had crashed the car or something equally traumatic. Fact is, your wife is paying very close attention to your actions even if she's giving you the cold shoulder.

Remember: you won't repair your relationship without putting in the time. First stop the bleeding, then start the healing.

Don't think you can rush things through. Relationship counselors follow a general rule of thumb that it takes about one month to change each year of dysfunction. In life, sports and relationships, the key to ultimate success is a desire to succeed (want-to), backed up by targeted skills and a strong helping of persistence and creativity.

The grand gesture

If you feel the relationship has soured so much that she is ready to end it, keep in mind the fallback of the grand gesture. In short, this is a major undertaking that tells her you really love her and are not going to stand by and just watch things end. The gesture may be a trip to Paris, quitting your beloved softball team, getting a different job, etc. Big moves like this can cause her to stop in her tracks and reconsider her opinion of you. However, do not assume this will work; it depends on your partner's personality and the level of damage already inflicted on the relationship. And once you do make a grand gesture, your game plan for change must be ready to go, as her faith will be at a low ebb and the demand for lasting improvement running high. In short, you may be in credibility overdraft.

My suggestion is this: no matter how negative your wife may be toward you, if you want the marriage to continue you should consider the grand gesture. You must let her know that you truly want to stay together. This may be your last hope for making her understand that you don't want to lose her. Keep in mind as you do this, however, that a woman's detachment may be too far along for the grand gesture to be effective.

Proceed with caution on the Hail Mary pass

In sales, bagging the big contract is called "landing the elephant." In reality, the elephant sale is a myth. The truth is that sales results are mostly dominated by a large number of small contracts. It's the same in football, where it's the short passes, good tackling and runs up the middle (the stuff that kept Doug Flutie an NFL star for so long) that bring in the wins. Similarly, in romance, the way forward is through small, consistent gains. Big, immediate results from your efforts to improve your romance/relationship skills, while welcome, are unlikely. Over the long-term, a once-in-a-lifetime trip for two to Timbuktu doesn't carry nearly as much weight with your wife as twenty smaller things you do for her regularly. It really depends on the level of crisis *right now* — and you're the only one who can gauge that.

Another analogy is the tortoise and the hare. In rekindling a romantic relationship with your wife, it is most likely that the tortoise will win the race. You're in this for the long haul, so don't get swayed by the lure of the quick fix. They rarely exist. And if it happens, my advice is to still follow through with the recommendations of this book. Develop patience as a skill. Throw those short completions, lots of them.

Fake it 'til you make it

One sense you may have right away in implementing changes is feeling like a fake. There's no question that once you confirm that she's the most important thing in your life you'll be making big changes in how you deal with your wife — changes that may seem foreign to both of you. At first, real change, whether in work, sports or relationships, can feel a little phony. Think of how a coach forced you to learn new techniques in your favorite sport and how awkward that felt. In relationships as well, new behaviors practiced over time become ingrained and begin to feel more natural.

Until then, it's worthwhile pretending to be comfortable with some of these activities — be a "genuine fake" — while you strive to make them your own. If you want to be a truly loving husband, faking it first cannot be viewed as a negative thing. It's the first step in changing your marriage technique into one that is positive for the relationship. While the faking may feel manipulative at first, keep the long-term goal in view.

Romance book? What book?

Does your woman need to know you are seeking guidance on being more loving? The answer is No. There's no harm in her thinking you're "naturally" romantic and that it "just comes more easily" to you than to other men. (She may even brag about you.) You need to retain some mystery in the relationship in order to protect its magic; too much information can throw cold water on still-hot — or at least lukewarm — coals.

Truth is, most of us aren't born romantic. For many men romance is an acquired skill, like working on a car engine or developing a smooth jumper. Romance must be learned, often through trial and error. In other words, although you should have educated yourself on this stuff with your girlfriends in your younger days, you probably didn't. Again, don't worry, you're not alone.

This reminds me of Clint Eastwood in the movie *Heartbreak Ridge*, where he plays a tough, macho military man who wants to get back together with his ex-wife. Having absolutely no idea how to woo her properly, he resorts to magazine articles on romance and delivers stilted efforts at being romantic that are almost embarrassing to watch. Fortunately, despite his buffoonery she sees through to the sincerity and honest effort he is making. The film has a happy ending, as movies tend to do. In the real world, while you're trying to avoid heartbreak ridge, it doesn't hurt to be a little smoother than this movie's hero.

That said, hopefully most women won't care if you had to read a book to get some tips on improving your relationship skills. They'll be much more impressed by the fact that you're making the effort for them.

Continue to do guy stuff

Although most men lean far too heavily to the male side, in moving toward a balanced lifestyle it is important not to tip too far the other way. So no matter how important rebuilding the relationship is to you, don't ever stop doing guy stuff such as sports, hunting, fishing, working on cars, etc. Don't neglect male activities or your friends. Maintain or even increase your male magnetism and personal power in areas like decision-making (being fair, not domineering), getting what you need, and protecting and providing for your family. While the John Wayne stereotype is obsolete, it's still likely your wife wants you to take charge once in a while, to be dominant rather than domineering, to be in control rather than controlling — most enjoy having somebody else make the decisions occasionally. The trick is knowing when to do this, and that involves paying attention to her moods with the current state of your relationship in mind. Hey, did I say this would be easy?

You may find that as you get more involved in the relationship that she'll be encouraging you to go out and do more guy stuff as a reward. Most women are very generous when their needs are being met!

Above all, use your gut instinct (aka intuition)

The above list of tips is just a selection of possibilities. Cookie-cutter approaches rarely work. For your efforts to be successful, you will need figure out whether a tip is appropriate to your situation. In this process, gut feel, combined with your feelings and experience, must be your guide. Try to visualize how each tip might work with your unique partner. Tweak the plan for maximum effectiveness. Connecting with your feelings, using your instincts, and combining your knowledge with appropriate strategies are the winning plays for improving your relationship.

CHAPTER 9

Your Game Plan

Building your unique playbook

———————————— ✷ ✷ ✷ ————————————

By now you've learned techniques for determining how you feel about your wife and how she may feel about you and the relationship. You have the tools to analyze where the relationship is at right now. With any luck you've taken the time to list the various things you do that may annoy her far out of proportion to the minimal effort that would be required by you to correct them. You probably have a great sense of the changes you need to make personally to improve your relationship.

Now let's go through a few exercises to help you establish a game plan that will fit the unique needs of your marriage. As in anything, the most important part of any game plan is to understand the situation and then address the challenges one by one. It's time to focus on developing an approach that will best utilize your hard preparatory work. A worksheet is provided below to help you in developing your game plan for success.

Keep in mind that your plan will need to be adjusted as you and your wife react to the changes you implement. For example, she may respond positively very quickly. The reverse may also occur. The key to winning at this effort will be your ability to sense the changes required and adapt your plan accordingly and as quickly as needed. This is the same as in football, basketball or any other strategy-based sport.

General rules for setting up your game plan

Take your time. You don't have to rush into things. As mentioned, your wife is an acute observer of your behavior. Any change, however positive, may be viewed with suspicion at first, depending upon the extent of marital breakdown.

Start by implementing the core competencies (deep listening, getting in shape, injecting a little humor, etc.) described earlier. These are the foundation of your new relationship skills — and for any relationship in your life, whether with children, friends or co-workers.

Then begin implementing the other tips you believe will enhance your relationship. Implement these in priority order of their positive impact on her. Use the 80/20 rule as your guide.

Evaluate her reactions (if any) and adjust your plan to fit. Tailor the speed of implementation according to the progress you see.

THE GAME PLAN PROCESS

1. Free up your mind and prepare for change.
2. Observe and thoroughly analyze your current state, and those of your wife and relationship.
3. Decide exactly what your game plan components will be and adjust as needed.
4. Execute the plan, keeping a close eye on her responses.
5. Adjust the plan according to the changing conditions.
6. Enjoy your improved relationship!

Note: If your relationship does not improve, then clearly you need to revise your game plan. The possible reasons for being unsuccessful are that you are expecting results too quickly, you're not being authentic in your changes (and she senses this) or you have underestimated her hard feelings toward you.

In any case, you need to take a fresh look at the situation to understand the true nature of your relationship — perhaps with a trusted advisor — and adjust your plan to suit that reality, however uncertain the outcome may be.

Be prepared for the worst

It's possible, despite all your efforts, that she may still want out. Perhaps of little comfort at the moment, at least you've avoided wasting further time on a doomed relationship.

How quickly should these changes be implemented?

This is a good question. The recommended course is to do the ones that will deliver the biggest bang for the buck immediately. Whatever you sense is most annoying to her, *stop doing it*. Then, perhaps, identify an element that's been lacking, and *start doing it*. Remember, psychologists say it takes a few weeks of repetition to make a new behavior a habit. Then undertake the tips that feel comfortable.

Bear in mind that continuity is vital: if you start a new habit (putting the toilet seat lid up and down and keeping the toilet clean) and then fall back into your old ways, you'll only have reinforced her poor opinion of you. Once you make a change, you can't go back. Stay centered and focused on your goals.

In terms of a time frame, implement these changes as quickly as seems appropriate. Every marriage game plan will be different, but you should look at taking between six months and two years to rebuild a faltering relationship. No matter what her response is, hang in there and don't quit too early. Remember, these changes are as much for you and your kids as they are for your wife.

Game plan worksheet

Go through the tips listed in the book and list those that could help your relationship:

_____

_____

_____

_____

_____

_____

_____

_____

Decide the order in which the changes should be implemented:

_____

_____

_____

_____

_____

_____

_____

Use the Notes section (page 139) if you need more room.

CHAPTER 10

It's Game Time

There is no "I" in team

※ ※ ※

Okay, this is the part where the coaches get a little nervous: it's time for the players to take over. Together, we've done the analysis of you, your wife and your relationship. You've reviewed your playbook and selected the plays that will help you best contribute to improving the team's fortunes. The game plan preparation is complete; now it's time to put it into action in real life. It's time to build a stronger relationship team.

I sincerely hope that separation is not in the cards for you. At the very least, I'm optimistic you've picked up a good understanding of what it takes for a man to be a successful player on a twenty-first century relationship team, where the two members are equals. It's really all about learning the skills needed to be a romantic partner and close friend. Breaking these skills down into manageable parts, as outlined, and then instituting them in your day-to-day life, is the best way to achieve this and avoid making the mistakes that can cause your spouse to walk away.

Remind yourself that (as in sports) it takes time to build a winning relationship team. Also, as in sports, there will be highs and lows along the way. Avoid making big pronouncements that will raise expectations; go with the subtle, self-assured actions we discussed earlier. How many times have we all heard teammates talk a mean game in the locker room and then not deliver on the court or field? Remember: less talk, more do. It's critical.

Now that you've formed a clear understanding of the specific challenges you face, and determined your level of want-to, success is within your grasp. Once you understand the relationship game and the skills and techniques that can give you an edge, you're on the right path. Most if not all of what you need is in this book and the recommended reading. Refer back to the Tips section frequently, and evaluate and change your game plan to suit evolving conditions.

For those of you who are competitive in sports, life and love, the bottom line is this: even if you implement only the fundamental improvements, you're well on the way to becoming the Jerry Rice of relationships. Apply the rest, and look out.

Well, what are you waiting for? It's game time. Go build a winning relationship team.

* * *

CLOSING COMMENTS

The researching and writing of this book have been invaluable to me personally. Although difficult at times — it's tough to revisit painful events — I have to say that I've learned a great deal about myself through the process. I now understand with wincing clarity how vital love relationships are to both men and women.

Although men don't like to admit it or even think about it all that much, having a healthy positive relationship is central to our health and happiness. It's one thing that I and millions of other men have discovered too late, to our regret. My sincere hope is that this book will help you and many others to avoid a similar fate.

Steve Campbell

APPENDIX: RECOMMENDED READING

GOOD ONES TO START WITH...

What Women Want Men to Know, Barbara De Angelis. Hyperion, 2001.

Getting Together and Staying Together — Solving the Mystery of Marriage, William Glasser, M.D., and Carleen Glasser. HarperCollins Publishers Inc., 2000.

How to Give Her Absolute Pleasure: Totally Explicit Techniques Every Woman Wants Her Man to Know, Lou Paget. Broadway Books, 2000.

The Five Love Languages: How to Express Heartfelt Commitment to Your Mate, Gary Chapman. Northfield Publishing, 1992. Men's version, published 2004.

1001 Ways to Be Romantic, Gregory Godek. Casablanca Press, 1999.

The RoMANtic's Guide — Hundreds of Creative Tips For a Lifetime of Love, Michael Webb. Hyperion, 2000.

Double Your Dating, David D'Angelo (www.doubleyourdating.com).

Men Are From Mars, Women Are From Venus (series of books), John Gray. HarperCollins, 1992.

No More Mr. Nice Guy: A Proven Plan For Getting What You Want in Love, Sex, and Life, Dr. Robert A. Glover. Running Press Book Publishers, 2000.

Relationship Rescue — A Seven-Step Strategy for Re-connecting With Your Partner, Phillip C. McGraw. Hyperion, 2000.

FOR A MORE IN-DEPTH VIEWPOINT...

Passionate Marriage Love, Sex, and Intimacy in Emotionally Committed Relationships, David Schnarch, Ph.D. Henry Holt & Co.

The Challenge of Marriage, Rudolf Dreikurs. M.D. Taylor & Francis, Third Edition, 1998.

The Mirages of Marriage, William J. Lederer and Don Jackson. W.W. Norton & Co., 1968.

The Parent's Handbook: Systematic Training for Effective Parenting (STEP), Don Dinkmeyer, Sr., Gary McKay, Don Dinkmeyer, Jr. American Guidance Services.

Mismatch: The Growing Gulf Between Women and Men, Andrew Hacker. Scribner, 2003.

The Road Less Traveled, M. Scott Peck. Touchstone Books, first published 1978.

Stiffed: The Betrayal of the American Male, Susan Faludi. HarperCollins, 1999.

The Meaning of Wife, Anna King. HarperCollins Canada, 2004.

ABOUT THE AUTHOR

Steve Campbell, BPE, MPE, APR, is a single father of two children and an accredited corporate communications and public relations consultant, writer and speaker. His background includes both a bachelor's and a master's degree in physical education, sports writing and reporting, and he is an active coach and volunteer in sports and community organizations. For information on relationship seminars and workshops in your area, please inquire at **www.thirdandlong.ca**.

NOTES

NOTES

NOTES

NOTES

NOTES

NOTES

Printed in the United States
25790LVS00002B/250-264